ALPHABET KILLER

ALPHABET KILLER

The True Story of the
Double Initial Murders

Cheri L. Farnsworth

STACKPOLE
BOOKS

Published by
STACKPOLE BOOKS
5067 Ritter Road
Mechanicsburg, PA 17055
www.stackpolebooks.com

Printed in the United States of America

10 9 8 7 6 5 4 3 2 1

FIRST EDITION

Library of Congress Cataloging-in-Publication Data

Farnsworth, Cheri, 1963–
  Alphabet killer : the true story of the double initial murders /
Cheri L. Farnsworth. — 1st ed.
      p. cm.
  Includes bibliographical references.
  ISBN-13: 978-0-8117-0632-2
  ISBN-10: 0-8117-0632-X
  1. Serial murders—New York (State)—Rochester—Case studies.
  2. Rape—New York (State)—Rochester—Case studies. I. Title.
  HV6534.R635F37 2010
  364.152'320974789—dc22
                                        2010014854

To three little angels
Carmen Colon
Wanda Walkowicz
Michelle Maenza

Introduction

Agatha Christie's *The A.B.C. Murders* is a classic detective novel about a serial killer whose victims' first and last names begin with the same initial—double initials—and live in towns beginning with the same letter. The killer murders his victims in alphabetical order, his first being Alice Ascher from Andover, his second Betty Barnard of Bexhill-on-Sea, and his third Carmichael Clarke from Churston. One can't help but notice the eerie similarity in the sound of Carmichael Clarke from Churston and Carmen Colon from Churchville, who became the first Double Initial victim. But the slayings in the greater Rochester, New York, area between 1971 and 1973, although seemingly similar in premise, did not progress alphabetically like they did in Christie's fiction. They went as follows: Carmen Colon near Churchville and Chili, Wanda Walkowicz in Webster, and Michelle Maenza in Macedon. Although the media attached much weight to the double initial aspect of the three murders, many investigators have downplayed its significance. Nevertheless, the coincidental double initials have become so strongly identified with the murders that the case is now known as the Double Initial Murders or the Alphabet Killings.

Located in the western Finger Lakes region on the southern shore of Lake Ontario, Rochester is New York's third largest metropolitan area, after New York City and Buffalo. The Greater Rochester area encompasses the counties of Monroe, Wayne, Genesee, Livingston, Ontario, and Orleans. The city proper lies within Monroe County. A retired Monroe County Sheriff's Office investigator, Sergeant Patrick Crough, describes a good many of the area's local sexual predators in his 2009 book *The Serpents Among Us*, including the still elusive Double Initial murderer, who is believed to be responsible for the murders of Carmen, Wanda, and Michelle. Several men have been questioned as suspects, either for all three murders or at least one of them.

Investigators know much more about the Double Initial homicides than they can say without compromising the integrity of the case. There is evidence that has never been divulged to the public, because the case has not been closed. Crough, although not at liberty to disclose information on recent DNA analyses and other forensic findings, was helpful in providing answers to questions fit for public consumption.

Modern forensics now allows investigators to use DNA comparisons on suspects, old and new, to either convict or exonerate them. The automated fingerprint identification system, a massive database used for criminal identification, had barely gotten up and running before Carmen's 1971 murder. Had the technology been available then, the murders of Carmen, Wanda, and Michelle might have been solved long ago. So the search for the killer goes on as forensics develop. This book provides a comprehensive timeline of the case.

CARMEN COLON

If ever a person could pass as a young Karen Carpenter, ten-year-old Carmen Colon was that girl. She was the spitting image. She had thick, long dark hair with bangs, dark eyes, and an easy, ready smile that could light up a room. Though she was born in Rochester, New York, in 1961, Carmen spent the first half of her life in her parents' native Puerto Rico. When the family returned to Rochester, Carmen, surrounded by Spanish-speaking relatives, struggled to learn English. She was placed in special education classes at the John Williams School No. 5 like countless other students who spoke Spanish as a first language, because the schools at the time lacked the resources to accommodate them. Even with this hurdle, Carmen had an upbeat, affable personality. The principal of her school, Dr. Alice Young, later told the press that Carmen was a "sweet little angel."

It was nearing dinnertime on November 16, 1971, when Carmen's mother, Guillonina, strode into her father-in-law's home, baby on hip. She stopped by often to visit. After all, she maintained strong ties to the family, even when Carmen's father, Justiniano, left them after they returned from Puerto Rico in the mid-1960s. His brother, Miguel Colon, later moved in with Guillonina and became her common-law husband. Carmen's "Uncle Miguel" then became her de facto stepfather. Carmen was one of six of Guillonina's children and she began floating between the home of her mother at 72 Romeyn Street and that of her paternal grandparents, Mr. and Mrs. Felix Colon, at 746 Brown Street. Only a ten-minute walk or three-minute drive separated the two houses. In the fall of 1971, Carmen was living with her grandparents, where she had her own bedroom, modestly adorned with religious décor, such as the crucifix she knelt before each night as she prayed for forgiveness—or perhaps for strength.

In a statement to Mark Starr of the Rochester *Democrat and Chronicle* on November 28, 1971, an unidentified uncle suggested that none of Carmen's aunts and uncles really cared for the girl or had much time for her. Perhaps that contributed to the frequent nightmares the same article said Carmen endured, some so disturbing that she fell right off her bed, as if struggling to escape the clutch of an unseen intruder. When the nightmares became the norm, according to the article, her grandparents stopped making their nightly trek down the hall to comfort her. Instead, she was left to her own devices to face a nocturnal nemesis that plagued her relentlessly and without pity.

When Guillonina popped in to visit her in-laws and see Carmen that fateful Tuesday, a nine-month-old daughter was ill and needed medicine from the nearby Jax Drugs store. It was a tough neighborhood with dope addicts roaming the streets, so Carmen's grandparents, stern Roman Catholics, preferred that their grandchildren stay within the confines of the metal gate encompassing the small front yard. Typically, according to an article in the *Democrat and Chronicle* of November 28, 1971, Felix Colon accompanied Carmen when she ran an errand or wanted to get a treat at the store, but it was becoming increasingly difficult for the old patriarch to keep up with his spirited granddaughter. On that day, however, Carmen begged to go alone. An exasperated Guillonina finally conceded after Felix assured her he would keep an eye on Carmen as she got the prescription filled for her stepsister. But Carmen didn't wait for Papa Felix to accompany her.

Eager to impress her mother with all the maturity a sixty-five-pound preteen can muster, Carmen laced up her white sneakers and threw on a long, red wool coat over green pants and a red-and-black sweater that some sources say was purple. She then bounded out the door at 4:25 P.M. into the chill November air. Within three or four minutes, she had reached the pharmacy in a shopping plaza two blocks away on the corner of West Main and Genesee streets, an area also known as Bull's Head because a stone statue of a bull's head overlooks the intersection. Carmen walked up to the counter and handed the pharmacist, Jack Corbin, the empty bottle, along with her mother's Medicaid card. Corbin told his pint-size patron that it would take half an hour to process the insurance and prepare the prescription, so Carmen said she'd be back. She seemed to be in a hurry. Then she was gone.

To this day, we can only speculate what may have transpired immediately after her brief exchange with Corbin. There was only one witness who ever came forward in both the preliminary and follow-up investigation. That witness reported seeing a child who looked like Carmen climbing into a car at dinnertime that day near Jax Drugs, but observed no struggle whatsoever. Nobody saw anything suspicious along the entire two-minute route between Jax Drugs and the Colon residence that day at the time in question.

By 5 P.M., when Carmen hadn't returned to either her grandparents' home or her mother's home, her mother became very concerned and sent an uncle out to look for her. By 7 P.M., concern within the extended Colon family had turned to alarm. They called the Rochester Police Department and more friends and relatives hit the streets in search of the ten-year-old child who was out there somewhere, alone in the dark in a rough section of the city—or so they thought. The urgency of the situation called for a methodical door-to-door search of the entire Bull's Head neighborhood, forty officers strong. But it was to no avail. What the searchers wouldn't know until it was far too late was that two hours before they were even notified of the missing child, at about 5:30 P.M., a girl matching Carmen's description was attempting a horrifying escape on Interstate 490 West.

Traffic on I-490 was barreling out of downtown Rochester at its usual rush-hour pace shortly before sunset that day. As drivers approaching Exit 3 to Churchville cranked up the volume to Jim Morrison and the Doors' ominous "Riders on the Storm" or tuned into the evening news about Phase 2 of President Nixon's plan to combat inflation, a young girl, naked from the waist down, suddenly appeared along the side of the highway racing toward oncoming traffic, eyes wide with terror and arms waving frantically. Closing in on the horrified child from behind was a car backing up, clearly hell-bent on catching her. "There's a killer on the road." Even as the lyrics imparted a subliminal warning to motorists only half listening at that moment, hundreds of cars sped past the desperate girl, and nobody stopped to help her.

In the seventies, there were no cell phones. No BlackBerries or pagers. There was no convenient way for motorists to get to a phone to call 911, the national emergency number that had just been created, to report a crime or emergency they had just witnessed on the interstate. I-490 is a thirty-seven-mile loop route that connects to the New York State Thruway at both ends. Although it serves metropolitan Rochester, cutting straight through the heart of the city on the Inner Loop Highway, Carmen Colon was seen running for her life in the rural Chili-Riga area, fifteen minutes southwest of central Rochester. She had been told at 4:30 to return in a half hour for the prescription, so her abductor must have picked her up outside the store sometime before 5 P.M. before heading onto I-490 West, where Carmen was seen making a break for it around 5:30. But vehicles along that stretch were whizzing past the girl at speeds up to seventy miles per hour en route to I-90, thinking only of leaving the city behind for the comforts of home after a long day of work.

Nobody made a single call about the girl they had seen until three days later, when her photograph appeared in the *Democrat and Chronicle* and the *Times-Union*, the city's two newspapers, which announced her brutal rape and murder. Even then, only a few individuals, out of the hundreds in cars estimated to have passed her on I-490, came forward to describe what they had seen. One said that while he thought it was odd that a young girl would be running half naked toward traffic on a busy highway, he was in the passing lane of heavy traffic when he saw her and thought for sure that someone behind him would stop to see if something was wrong. Another insisted he thought the car he saw backing up toward the child was just allowing her out to go to the bathroom. Some people thought it was perhaps a family squabble that was none of their business. Others were unsure of what they had seen, either because it was too much of a blur in the drizzle as they sped past with their minds on other things, or because it was already pretty dark as the crescent moon yielded precious little light on an already surreal scene. So those individuals put the disturbing image out of their minds and continued on.

Although the handful of witnesses that admitted to seeing Carmen that night gave varying descriptions of the vehicle backing up toward her, one said it looked just like the brand-new car thirty-seven-year-old Miguel Colon, Carmen's stepfa-ther-uncle, had just purchased. Miguel, who years later committed suicide after attempting to shoot Guillonina, had been a prime suspect from the start. Based on tips that con-tinue to filter in to this day (even from anonymous Colon family members), he still is. But there were at least six different descriptions given for the vehicle that passersby saw on the side of the highway that night, and only one matched Miguel's. Another witness saw Carmen being led back to the car by a man holding her arm and reasoned that the girl didn't seem to be trying to get away, so he didn't consider it an emergency. By that point, she had likely either expended every last ounce of energy in her futile attempt to escape her killer, leaving her too depleted to offer any resistance by the time he caught up to her, or the assailant threatened to kill her right then and there if she didn't get back into the car.

"No One Stopped!"

"Apathy Abounds as Motorists Ignore Girl"

"Nobody Stopped to Save Carmen"

"Girl is Slain after Motorists Ignore Her Pleading for Help"

"Hundreds Saw Carmen, No Motorist Stopped"

Those were just a few of the countless headlines in newspapers across the nation in the last half of November 1971. People were shocked and baffled to think that nobody stopped to help a little girl in trouble on the side of a busy highway. But that year, when the Child Abuse Reporting Law had just been enacted to protect and identify abused children, strangers were far more reluctant to file reports of suspicious activity than they are today. Thus, those few individuals who came forward several days later and admitted to seeing Carmen running on I-490 were not admonished by local authorities for their failure to stop. Rather, the lead investigator at the time, Monroe County chief sheriff's detective Michael Cerretto, said he could understand why some people might have continued driving, according to a widely distributed Associated Press news article written by Ben DeForest.

It was already pretty dark out, making it difficult to see much on the side of the road, especially when driving 65 miles per hour. So it's likely some of the motorists who drove past the incident failed to notice something was awry. Social psychologist Victor Harris, then of the University at Buffalo (UB), offered a theory based on his own research. He said it was a classic case of a social psychological occurrence known alternatively as crowd apathy, the bystander effect, diffusion of responsibility, and the Genovese Syndrome.

This phenomenon occurs when individuals witness an emergency but are reluctant to help if other people are present. The more witnesses there are to a crisis, the less likely any one individual will be to step in and offer assistance, because they erroneously assume that there is no emergency if others around them are also ignoring it. They believe that if help is warranted, then surely someone else will take the appropriate course of action, because so many others are also aware of it. Both ideas release any given individual from feeling solely responsible for the outcome of an emergency situation. In other words, the diffusion of responsibility makes it easier for them to live with themselves afterward.

Every generation seems to have a case of crowd apathy that makes the news and stuns the nation. Before the Carmen Colon tragedy of 1971, the most famous of these was the stabbing death of Kitty Genovese in Queens, New York, in 1964. In that incident, the twenty-nine-year-old woman was attacked by a knife-wielding man when she returned home from work early one morning. Several neighbors heard her screams as the man repeatedly stabbed her in the back. Some even witnessed the crime. Yet only one spoke up and yelled for the attacker to stop, which he did briefly. Genovese staggered alone toward her apartment, collapsing outside of a locked door. Ten minutes later, the brazen killer returned and continued raping and stabbing her for a full half hour until she was dead. It was estimated that twelve to thirty-eight people saw or heard the lethal attacks, but as in the case of Carmen, not one came to her rescue. The public was outraged, especially after reading a *New York Times* article two weeks after the incident called "Thirty-Eight Who Saw Murder Didn't Call the Police." The fact is nobody knows exactly how many people saw the crime taking place. It may have been less or it may have been more. Some who did see it may have been too ashamed or fearful of public ridicule to come forward as witnesses after hearing of Genovese's fate. The Genovese case inspired important psychological research regarding crowd apathy.

Although it seems a scenario like this could never happen today in an age of instant communication, it happened as recently as 2009 in two well-publicized incidents. The first was when a woman in her twenties was brutally raped by a panhandler in broad daylight in a park in Spokane, Washington, as hundreds of witnesses, including many children, either watched or listened to her screams with apparent disregard. The other was when a fifteen-year-old California girl leaving her high school homecoming dance was brutally gang-raped and beaten. The attack left the young girl in critical condition. For more than two hours, some twenty witnesses either watched or took part. Although word quickly spread about what was happening outside on school property, not a single individual called 911 or did anything to help the girl until her battered, unconscious body was later found under a bench.

In Carmen's case, anyone could have turned off on Exit 3, past the Black Creek Bridge, to find a pay phone; or better yet, go to the fire and rescue squad just seconds down the street in the village of Churchville. Instead they assumed that someone else would surely do what their own conscience asked of them. Should I or shouldn't I? With an understandable fear of endangering themselves and others in a multicar pileup by slamming on their brakes in the dense traffic to see what was going on, and with too little time to comprehend what they were seeing to even formulate the appropriate split-second reaction to it, they instead left it in the hands of those behind them, hoping for the best, and drove past the little girl who was about to be savagely raped, beaten, and strangled to death.

On November 18, two days after Carmen's disappearance, her horribly battered body was discovered in a ditch by two boys, fifteen-year-old Mark Allen of Churchville and thirteen-year-old James Gillen of Clifton. The isolated area where the body was found is technically in the town of Riga, according to town clerk Kimberly Pape, but it is in close proximity to the village of Churchville and the Chili town border. An article in the *Times-Union* on November 19, 1971, said the teens were on a bike ride on Griffin Road and had just turned left onto the sparsely populated Stearns Road, a mile from the Chili border, when they spotted what they thought was a plastic "broken doll" crumpled against a boulder on the side of the road. Closer inspection revealed the body of an actual child wearing nothing but a sweater, blue socks, and white sneakers, just like the girl seen on I-490 W. It was 4:30 P.M., exactly forty-eight hours since Carmen left Jax. With darkness looming, the body was removed for autopsy, and spotlights were set up in the fields to accommodate an initial search for clues. The next day a more thorough search resumed, and Carmen's coat was found in a culvert about three hundred feet from her body, where it looked as if it had been tossed out of the fleeing car as an afterthought. Eleven days later, her green pants were found near a service road one mile before Exit 3 on I-490, right where witnesses had seen the car and the girl running, confirming that the girl they had seen that night was, in fact, Carmen Colon. The discovery of the pants led to the theory that Carmen had either interrupted a rape attempt or that she had already been raped before she made a run for it. Where she was actually killed remains a mystery. It may have been near the highway where she was last seen, near the rock on Stearns Road where her body was found, or somewhere else altogether. It seems likely that it was on Stearns Road, because the killer had to have been so taken aback by Carmen's potentially incriminating actions that he just wanted to grab her and get off the interstate before someone stopped or came back. There's no way he would have remained at the scene of that incident any longer after he got her back into the car.

Carmen's uncles, Angelo and Julio (but not Miguel), identified their niece's battered body. Angelo told Associated Press correspondent Ben DeForest that he could see "dried tears on her cheeks." Monroe County medical examiner, Dr. John Edland, conducted the autopsy and determined that Carmen had been raped, beaten, and strangled to death. Severe bruising and what appeared to be human fingernail scratches covered her slim little body. Edland also found that she had suffered fractures to the skull and the area about the neck in the ferocious attack. In the end, the little girl who had so valiantly fought off an abusive fiend in her sleep night after night ended up dying at the hands of a monster who stepped right out of her worst nightmare.

Funeral services for Carmen were held first at her mother's house on Romeyn Street at 8:30 A.M. and then at Saints Peter and Paul Roman Catholic Church at 9 A.M. on November 22, 1971. An estimated two hundred people attended the Spanish-language service. Following the funeral, with snow gently falling, Carmen was laid to rest in the Holy Sepulchre Cemetery on Lake Avenue.

While the grieving family was preoccupied with Carmen's funeral arrangements and burial, an exhaustive murder investigation was underway by the Monroe County Sheriff's Office and the New York State Police, the lead investigative agencies in the case. But the entire Rochester community rolled up their sleeves and offered assistance. Gannett Rochester Newspapers, owner of the city's *Times-Union* and *Democrat and Chronicle* morning and afternoon papers, set up a $2,500 reward fund, along with a witness line for people to call with tips. Readers were also encouraged to submit tips to the paper by mail. All tips received, and there were many, were turned over to the police. Other businesses and private individuals added to the reward fund until it eventually grew to more than $6,000. In February 1972, an organization called Citizens for a Decent Community came up with the ingenious idea of placing five billboards around Bull's Head to keep interest in the case alive. The signs immediately generated more tips.

Ten days into the murder investigation, police had already picked up and questioned hundreds of people, including known sex offenders in the area. Yet, with the exception of the motorists passing Carmen on I-490 and the one individual who saw her enter a vehicle at Bull's Head, nobody else had seen anything substantial. There was an ominous development described in the *Democrat and Chronicle* on November 21, 1971, however, in an article called "Can You Help Find a Killer?" It said that on the sixth floor of a building at 228 East Main Street, which was then occupied by the Sibley, Lindsay & Curr department store, someone had written a note on the wooden men's room door saying, "I killed a 10-year-old girl. Who will be next?" Sibley's was less than two miles, or a five-minute drive, from the houses of Carmen's grandparents and mother.

For most of the first month, a dozen detectives and officers were assigned primarily to the Colon case. By late December, however, Cerretto, who was heading the manhunt, decided that they were caught up with all of the leads, having questioned individuals from every home and business in the Bull's Head area at least once. There was no longer justification for keeping so many men on the case full-time. So December 21, 1971, the size of the force assigned to the case full-time was decreased to three very capable Monroe County sheriff's detectives who were tasked with pursuing new leads and double-checking previous information. Once the billboards with Carmen's school portrait were placed around the area two months later, the leads increased substantially, so that by April of 1972, five months after the crime, the number of people questioned in Carmen's murder had purportedly grown to a thousand.

Many of the individuals questioned in the Carmen Colon murder case were family, friends, acquaintances, business owners and employees in the Bull's Head neighborhood; but officers also questioned known sex offenders living in Rochester, especially in that southwest section of the city. There are several types of child abduction. Most common by far is when a non-custodial parent steals their child from the other parent, usually during or following divorce proceedings. When strangers abduct children, it is generally for one of three reasons: to abuse, torture, or murder the child; to get ransom for the child; or to keep the child as their own. In the Double Initial murders, the three victims were presumably abducted for the purpose of sexually abusing them. Whether murder was originally part of the killer's plan became irrelevant the moment he crossed that line.

Scores of books have been written about pedophiles and child predators, but they rarely cover sex offenders who kill. In Carmen's case, we may never know if the person responsible for her murder planned to kill her when he abducted her, or if he snapped after her unanticipated attempt to escape and realized she had been this close to exposing him. It is unknown if Carmen's was a single, isolated sexual assault gone horribly wrong or if the killer was a repeat offender who had raped and possibly murdered young children both before Carmen's slaying and after. It is uncertain whether Carmen knew her abductor or if he was a complete stranger. All we can presume is that she went willingly with him from Jax Drugs, because apparently nobody saw anything amiss at the busy intersection that day. The only potential witness to Carmen's abduction said she thought she saw Carmen climbing into a car parked outside of the pharmacy where she was last seen and that she appeared to be doing so willingly.

Patrick Crough is a retired investigator sergeant from the Monroe County Sheriff's Office Major Crimes Unit. In that capacity he investigated murders, rapes, assaults, crimes against children, and other serious felonies. He was the commander of the Monroe County Sheriff Hostage Rescue Team and has worked undercover in the Violent Warrant Squad, the Vice Squad, the Narcotics Unit, and a firearms suppressions unit, targeting violent criminals who were trafficking illegal firearms in the Rochester area.

Crough was also the lead investigator in the Double Initial murders and wrote *The Serpents Among Us* to detail his firsthand knowledge and perspective of this and other cases involving children. Published by the nonprofit Millstone Justice Children's Advocacy Organization, the book is an altruistic effort on behalf of a veteran investigator to educate parents about how to recognize a child predator and take proactive steps to protect children. Crough divides sex offenders into three categories based on his own contact with such individuals over the course of the past twenty years. These categories, however, are often used interchangeably in other sources and especially in the media.

Pedophiles are people who fantasize about having sex with children. They may or may not ever act on that impulse. They often appear to be normal family men holding down decent jobs and respectable positions within the community. Yet, even their own relatives and coworkers may never realize the dark secrets these men harbor, until they get caught. In August 2003, for example, a military police officer at West Point sent nude photographs of himself to a thirteen-year-old girl before arranging a meeting at a restaurant where he was busted, according to a special report in the *Daily News* on November 1, 2003. An elementary school teacher with "a sterling reputation" in the Bronx pleaded guilty to emailing child pornography photographs to an undercover agent in 2001. Most who sexually abuse preteens like Carmen are pedophiles.

All it takes is one irreversible act to be labeled a *child molester*, the second sex offender group Crough describes. Once that line has been crossed and a man has been found guilty of sexually assaulting a child, the label will remain with him forever, even if he never repeats the offense. A United States Department of Justice study on *recidivism*, the act of repeating an offense even after having been punished or treated for it, found that six out of seven criminals incarcerated for sex crimes, including those against children, were first-time offenders. Child molesters are not necessarily pedophiles, although some esteemed organizations like the Mayo Clinic estimate that ninety-five percent of them are; pedophiles are not necessarily child molesters, unless they act on their urge. The Mayo study, "A Profile of Pedophilia: Definition, Characteristics of Offenders, Recidivism, Treatment Outcomes, and Forensic Issues," by Ryan and Richard

Hall, said that pedophilic child molesters commit ten times more sex acts against children than non-pedophilic child molesters. Child molesters who are not pedophiles typically prefer adult sex, but for whatever reason, molest a child, whether for instant gratification at the expense of a helpless victim who happens to be at the wrong place at the wrong time, out of some morbid curiosity exacerbated perhaps by drugs or alcohol, or to get revenge on one of the victim's relatives.

Ninety percent of child molesters are acquainted with their victim. Of that number, thirty percent are relatives—fathers, stepfathers, brothers, uncles, grandfathers, or cousins. The rest are people like babysitters, neighbors, and friends of the family. Only ten percent are strangers. At the time of the Double Initial murders, warnings to children emphasized the danger of strangers rather than familiar family members and friends. Many news articles published then stressed the efforts the Rochester City School District made to ensure that every elementary student in their schools received age-appropriate training about "stranger danger." The school had done its part, to the best of its ability based on recommendations at the time. And yet Carmen, and later, Wanda and Michelle, were still plucked off the city streets in the late afternoon with no apparent struggle. Were they part of the ninety percent of children who know their molesters? Molesters are opportunists who target vulnerable, unprotected children for any number of personal reasons, and the vast majority of the victims know their attacker.

The final category of sex offenders in Crough's book is the *child predator*. A child predator is just what the term implies—an animal hunting for prey, with the prey being the most trusting, defenseless creature on earth, a child. When a predator sets his sights on a particular child, he will formulate a plan to gain access to that child and will often expend much time and money toward that effort. These offenders are often otherwise upstanding citizens like teachers, politicians, Boy Scout leaders, babysitters, day-care workers, youth ministers, or camp counselors. They tend to put down roots in their community and present an honorable face to neighbors, coworkers, and even their own families, wiggling their way into a vulnerable child's life under the guise of being a helpful adult.

According to a report called "Profiles of Sexual Predators and Reducing the Risk of Sexual Misconduct at Your Church, School or Other Youth Organization" prepared by attorney F. Robert Radel II, there are at least twenty-six common traits of career molesters or predators. Radel says that "pedophilic child molesters" are often single, over twenty-five years old, and don't date, because they have trouble performing sexually with adults when their preference is clearly children. They often live alone or with their parents, but if they choose to marry as a cover for their secret obsession with children as sex objects, they often marry a "passive woman-child" with little sexual experience or expectations. They may have been discharged from the military if their penchant for child pornography became known. They continually attempt to gain access to vulnerable children, finding ways to socialize with youngsters on their own turf. Socialization with adult friends, on the other hand, may often be sorely lacking in the lives of child predators, unless their friends share their sickness. Most pedophiles prefer children of a certain age and sex and are adept at targeting those who are most vulnerable. Victims, according to Radel, are often from broken homes and low-income families, like Carmen and the subsequent Double Initial victims. The predator may see them as neglected and lonely, and thus, more willing to accept his affections.

Carmen, Wanda, and Michelle were victims of molestation in the gravest sense of the word, and they may fit into Radel's comprehensive picture of the typical child molester and his victim. But what causes a child molester to not only abduct and violate his victim, but to then murder the child? Fear of being exposed is probably the biggest factor, considering that ninety percent of molesters could be identified by their victims. Some may go on a power trip or make it part of their sexual fantasy to take a child's virginity and life simultaneously. And some may murder a hysterical young victim screaming in agony to silence them, so they can finish the sex act without drawing attention to themselves. Kenneth V. Lanning is the author of *Child Molesters: A Behavioral Analysis for Law-Enforcement Officers Investigating the Sexual Exploitation of Children by Acquaintance Molesters* and a thirty-year FBI veteran who spent two-thirds of his career in the Behavioral Science Unit and National Center for the Analysis of Violent Crime at the FBI Academy. He revised the old typology of child molesters to create a more concise and accurate picture of sex offenders who target children. Three types stand out as most relevant to the Double Initial murders: the situational-type, morally indiscriminate; the situational-type, inadequate; and the preferential-type, sadistic.

Situational-type molesters do not have an exclusive preference for children; thus, they are not necessarily pedophiles. They may victimize anyone who is vulnerable: the disabled, the elderly, or the ill, for example. Typically, they have fewer child victims (sometimes only one) than preferential-type child molesters, who by definition prefer only children. The *morally indiscriminate* situational molester has little conscience. There are few boundaries he has not crossed. He may physically, psychologically, or sexually abuse those with whom he works, lives, or sees socially. He lies and steals as often as he is able or inclined to, and he molests young children, simply because he can. When the sexual urge strikes, regardless of where he is, he chooses a child based on opportunity and availability, and he uses physical force or manipulation to reel them in. This type of molester frequently targets strangers and acquaintances, but he also may target his own biological children, stepchildren, or the children of a live-in girlfriend.

Inadequate situational molesters (ISMs) have what Lanning calls "low social competence," so they often appear to be painfully shy or eccentric. These men molest children out of curiosity and insecurity, having had little, if any, sexual experience with other adults. The ISM chooses children and the elderly as his victims, because he does not find them to be sexually threatening. Because of the ISM's propensity to let unprocessed feelings of anger and hostility fester, he often reaches a point of exploding, and that's when he is most likely to strike, taking his wrath out on a victim in the form of a violent sexual assault or torture, and sometimes murder. The most important point to be made about the two sub-types of situational-type child molesters described above is that they are responsible for the majority of sexually motivated child murders. Lanning is quick to point out, however, that any child molester could become capable of murder in order to avoid identification.

Preferential-type child molesters (PTCMs) are typically pedophiles, because they obsessively fantasize about and show a definite inclination toward sex acts with preadolescent children. While situational molesters victimize children simply because they can—or because they had a bad day, snapped, and took it out on the nearest vulnerable person available—PTCMs molest young children because those are the only individuals they are sexually attracted to. Thus, preferential-type molesters molest children in greater numbers and with far greater frequency than do situational types. Lanning further separated this category into four patterns of preferential molestation: seduction, introverted, sadistic, and diverse. Carmen's killer demonstrated shades of the sadistic preferential-type child molestation.

It can be argued that all child molesters are sadistic. Lanning puts the *sadistic* preferential-type child molesters in a category of their own. He describes them as individuals whose arousal stems from their victim's instinctive response to the psychological and physical pain inflicted upon them by their molester. The sadistic molester lures or forces his victim into his trap and is more likely to choose someone unknown to him to avoid being later identified. This next point is key: If this type of molester does "engage in severe sexual sadism" with a child acquaintance or family member, Lanning says, it would be difficult to escape identification without killing the victim. Thus, sadistic child molesters are more likely than any of the other four preferential-type child molesters to abduct and murder a child.

Child molesters who kill their victims have a much higher rate of suicide than the other types, according to Lanning. Much of this may have to do with lifetimes of abuse and personality disorders. But, in some cases, perhaps they are haunted by their crimes until they can no longer take it. Maybe the only way they feel they can end the insanity that causes them to kill is by killing themselves before they strike again. Or maybe they prefer death to what would await them in prison if they were ever incarcerated, choosing instead to take their own lives rather than assume the position of child killers and child molesters at the bottom of the food chain in prison.

There were two primary suspects in Carmen's death the first year: Miguel Colon and James Barber. Colon was both her uncle and her common-law stepfather. He became a leading suspect in late February 1972 after a New York City resident saw an article in the paper about the billboards that Citizens for a Decent Community had put up. The man told sheriff's detective sergeants Donald Clark and Nicholas DeRosa that Miguel had shown up at his place shortly after Carmen's murder, saying he needed to get out of the country quick, because he had "done something wrong in Rochester," according to a *Times-Union* article written by Dick Cooper and Jim Sykes on March 16, 1972. Five days later, a *Democrat and Chronicle* article added that it was unclear if the man knew what his friend's transgressions were before he read the article in a Spanish newspaper, but Carmen's name had been specifically mentioned to him. Suddenly, the media came alive with a flurry of reports regarding an unidentified suspect's hasty departure to Puerto Rico and Monroe County district attorney Jack Lazarus's pursuit of him.

Along with Lazarus, the two sheriff's detectives who interviewed the New York City informant, an interpreter, and a stenographer all flew to San Juan where they were assisted by Capt. Hector Lugo, Puerto Rican Chief of Detectives. But news articles published in Rochester and on the front page of the *San Juan Star*, with the latter saying "N.Y. Police Seek Girl's Slayer Here," preceded the arrival of Lazarus and company, giving Miguel a very good reason to hide in the jungle for the entire six days that the investigators were there. When they questioned his friends and family in San Juan, they were told Miguel was armed and had "gone underground," according to the *Times-Union* of March 22, 1972. Lazarus later claimed that the news media had spoiled his manhunt, saying the papers had been instructed not to publicize the trip to Puerto Rico because it could jeopardize the authorities' case. Stuart Dunning, executive director of the *Democrat and Chronicle* and *Times-Union*, countered that the tip and the trip had been known in Rochester for weeks, so they were not the whistleblowers as far as they were concerned. Indeed, some of Miguel's family members in Rochester had also been questioned about his activities well before the Rochester contingent departed for Puerto Rico. Regardless of whose fault it was that Miguel found out he was being pursued, the group returned to Rochester empty-handed.

Plan B involved detaining Miguel's elderly mother and doing a little impromptu media blitz to announce that she would remain in jail until her son came out of hiding and agreed to cooperate. That did the trick. Miguel was flown back to Rochester for questioning, with the assurance that his mother would be released, according to Crough. He said that although some detectives felt strongly (and still do) that Miguel had abducted, raped, and strangled Carmen, Lazarus decided at the time that there was not enough evidence to convict him. Yes, a witness had described a vehicle like Miguel's new car backing up toward the girl she saw running along I-490. Yes, Miguel's car appeared to have been cleaned both inside and in the trunk right before police got to it. Yes, he had left the Rochester area in a hurry right after Carmen was killed, which may explain why he didn't identify the body and why he wasn't in the newspaper photo with his parents and brothers that ran the day after Carmen's body was found. And yes, Carmen knew him. But he maintained his innocence throughout the six-hour interrogation and managed to pass a lie detector test taken at the state police headquarters in Canandaigua, New York. Lie detector tests, however, can lie. They are not admissible in court because of the longstanding debate about their accuracy.

Cerretto had no choice but to release Miguel on March 28, 1972, saying there was no further need to question him. Retired investigator DeRosa recently told the *Democrat and Chronicle* he was disappointed that it wasn't left to a grand jury to decide if Miguel could be indicted. With the prime suspect out of the picture, DeRosa said leads in the case all but ceased. According to Crough's book, he still believes Miguel was Carmen's rapist and murderer, regardless of the results of the polygraph test.

Some investigators today believe there may be a "deep-seated secret" within the Colon family regarding Miguel's involvement. They had trouble getting straight answers from his family over the years, according to one senior investigator. Comments about Miguel's behavior that were recently made by one of his close relatives to police strongly implicate him in the murder. If he was innocent, why was Miguel Colon running to the jungles of San Juan? What prompted him to hide until forced out by shame, when his mother was used as bait?

On February 17, 1991, nearly twenty years after Carmen was killed, Miguel Colon shot himself to death in a house on Radio Street after assaulting Carmen's mother, Guillonina, and Guillonina's brother, Juan Melendez, with the same gun during a domestic dispute. When police arrived, Miguel demanded to be shot. When those demands were not met, he shot and killed himself then and there, taking many unanswered questions to the grave with him. Investigators Crough and Tom Vasile interviewed Guillonina and Juan, wondering if perhaps a self-incriminating deathbed statement had been made before Miguel ended his life, but they denied any such admission of guilt had been made by the deceased.

The other primary suspect in the Carmen Colon case was James Barber. According to Crough's book, Monroe County sheriff investigator Sgt. Robert Russello found a connection when he learned that Barber had already been arrested for molesting a young girl in the past and was, at the time of Carmen's murder, wanted for assaulting and sodomizing a fifteen-year-old girl in Ohio. He happened to be in the Bull's Head neighborhood, where he "had social ties," when she was abducted and killed. *Democrat and Chronicle* staff writer Gary Craig has done extensive research on the case, and along with videographer Max Schulte, prepared an impressive, interactive special report on the Double Initial murders for the newspaper's online edition. Craig said that Barber worked in the Bull's Head area and had penciled in his hours on his time card the day Carmen disappeared, rather than letting the machine punch the information in. There is no indication that the penciled scribbling on his time card was ever compared to the penciled scribbling on the men's room door that police found in the city a few days after Carmen's murder. Even more suspiciously, Barber left his job without notice right after Carmen's body was found and apparently left the Rochester area so quickly that he never bothered to take his belongings from his apartment with him. Sergeant Russello pursued the lead, but the trail ran cold and the suspect is now deceased. Because Barber left the area after Carmen's murder and apparently never returned, he is not implicated in either of the other Double Initial Murders.

WANDA WALKOWICZ

Wanda was a red-headed, blue-eyed, and freckle-faced child who lived in the north-central part of Rochester. At eleven, she was mature beyond her years, all sixty-five pounds of her, fussing over her curly pixie haircut like a teen and playing outside with friends until late on weekends. Wanda was born on August 4, 1961, to Joyce and Richard Walkowicz, but Richard died of a heart attack at the age of thirty when Wanda was just six years old and her little sister Rita was five. A year later, Joyce, a pretty young mother sporting a deep auburn bouffant, moved herself and her two fair-haired girls into an upstairs apartment in a brown, two-story clapboard house at 132½ Avenue D off Conkey. There, they struggled to survive on the few hundred dollars Joyce received monthly from her husband's social security benefits. Not only was the living arrangement on Avenue D affordable, but it was conveniently located just three blocks from the school that Rita and Wanda attended. It was also in the area of a few bars that Joyce patronized. In the years following Richard's death, Joyce found relief from her woes in the neighborhood taverns, often taking Wanda and Rita with her to keep an eye on them, while maintaining some semblance of a social life. Sometime after another daughter, Michelle, came along, Peyton "Junior" Raney moved in and became Joyce's common-law husband, providing a stint of stability to the family's lifestyle.

April 2, 1973, was a cold, wet day in Rochester, but that didn't dampen Wanda's mood as she raced home from School 8 on the corner of Avenue A and Conkey with her best report card ever. Even after missing fifty-seven days of school that year, her fifth-grade teacher said she was "an average student, a little above average in reading," according to an article published in the *Times-Union* two days later. Joseph Hillmon wrote on Wanda's permanent school record that she was very neat and diligent in her studies, and he gave her two "outstandings" for behavior. Not only was she a good little worker, but article after article said she was a happy, personable child, well-liked by all. Wanda's teacher told the media that he could sense Wanda had many responsibilities at home, but it never seemed to bother her. In fact, she seemed to bask in the role of the "little mom" or a "mini-adult," as Investigator Crough called her.

Wanda was street-smart and quite capable of caring for her mother and sisters, if needed. By the time they were ten and eleven, Wanda and Rita had both became accustomed to interrupting their play to run errands for their mother, walking alone through their lower-middle-class neighborhood.

Sometimes they went together or with a friend. But more often than not, Wanda went alone if it was her turn to do so, regardless of the weather. Necessities were needed that Monday evening. The family pets were out of food, two-year-old Michelle was out of diapers, and they needed basics like bread and milk for dinner. So about 5:10 P.M., Joyce asked Wanda to drop what she was doing and run to the Hillside Delicatessen at 213 Conkey Avenue. Her coloring book would still be there when she got back. It was her turn to go.

The deli was just past Wanda's school three blocks away, so it was certainly a familiar route to her. She could probably have walked it blindfolded by then. At least twice a day, she walked past the duplexes, apartment buildings, barbershop, stores, and bars that lined Conkey Avenue between her house and the school and deli at Avenue A. It only took four minutes if she didn't get distracted along the way. Thus, dressed in the blue-and-white-checked dress, white socks, and sneakers she had worn to school that day, "the little redhead of Avenue D," as the *Democrat and Chronicle* called her, headed out the door. One of the first news articles regarding Wanda mentioned that she was wearing a green and red coat. Later articles stated that she was not wearing a coat at all. She saw three friends who lived nearby as they were heading to a different store and walked with them to the corner of Conkey and Avenue D. By then, the air outside had dipped to 45.9 degrees, and a steady rain made it feel even colder, especially on Wanda's thin bare legs. Nevertheless, she arrived at Hillside and dutifully picked up every item on her list: two quarts of milk, a package of disposable diapers, bread, cupcakes, soup, tuna fish, dog food, and cat food. While bagger William

Van Orden crammed everything into one overloaded paper sack so that the child would have only a single bag to carry home, store clerk Richard Checchi jotted down the total of $8.52 in Joyce's brown charge book. Checchi said that everything seemed normal that day. All Wanda said to him was, "I'm in a hurry," likely because her mother had told her to hurry back home, nothing more. The clerk said it was not unusual for Wanda to say something like that.

Store employees, two male customers, and a third individual standing outside the store all saw Wanda leave Hillside carrying the bulky bag between 5:15 and 5:30. She was heading north on Conkey toward home. A woman who once babysat for Joyce was sitting at Jimmie's Tavern across the street from Hillside when she saw Wanda leaving the deli. She considered scooting outside with her umbrella to accompany her former charge home, but decided against it; Wanda seemed to be doing just fine. The three kids who had walked with Wanda to the corner of Avenue D looked down Conkey as they came out of their store, just as Wanda departed Hillside. She was a couple blocks behind them, and since it was raining, they didn't wait for her to catch up. The next time they looked back, they saw her leaning against the school fence, struggling to get a better grip on the heavy bag. A moment later, they glanced back again, and Wanda was gone—and so was a big brown car they had just seen approaching from the same direction that Wanda was walking. It must have turned off on one of the side streets.

The Walkowiczes were regulars at Hillside, and Joyce knew exactly how long it took for her daughters to walk to the store, pick up groceries, and return home. When that amount of time had elapsed, Wanda sent Rita to the store to see what the holdup was. Rita's friend, twelve-year-old Franciene Eiskamp, joined her. On their way, the girls stopped at the homes of two of Wanda's friends to see if she was there, but she wasn't and hadn't been. Then around 6:45 P.M., they got to the Hillside deli and asked if Wanda had been in to purchase groceries yet. Rita was handed a copy of the receipt for the groceries confirming that her sister had picked up everything on the list and left. Still not thinking anything sinister had occurred, Rita purchased two bagfuls of additional items, in case Wanda didn't get home in time for dinner, and headed home to let Joyce know that they didn't find Wanda.

At 7:47 P.M., two and a half hours since she had last seen her daughter, Joyce called the Rochester Police Department to report Wanda missing, and then she headed to the delicatessen herself to query the employees about her eldest daughter's visit. Like Rita, Joyce then went to the houses of Wanda's best friends in a futile, frantic effort to find her daughter. By 8:15, a massive search and rescue was underway. Police and neighbors were searching backyards, alleys, the railroad tracks, and the entire area between the tracks and Avenue A.

While taking the missing persons report, police were told of a close encounter Wanda and a nine-year-old friend had two nights earlier with a strange man near the railroad tracks a block away at around 10 P.M. When a stranger chased them, the girls started running, and the man jumped into the bushes. They hadn't seen his face, but they got a glimpse of his shoes with buckles on them. It turned out that the man was a known sex offender. Joyce was asked by police if she was aware of the incident and admitted remorsefully that she was.

Bernie Conversi, a director at a local recreation center on the other side of the railroad tracks that Wanda frequented on pleasant summer days, told police he thought he had seen Wanda on that side of the tracks at 7 P.M. on the night she vanished. Why would she walk in the rain from the deli, past her own house, and then continue to the other side of the railroad tracks a block farther, carrying a heavy bag of items her mother needed right then? Like many other tips offered at the time, it was offered with good intentions but made little sense.

Tuesday morning should have been a time of celebration in the Walkowicz household. It was Rita's tenth birthday. But nobody had slept a wink the night before, and the friends and family that surrounded Rita and her mother were not there to celebrate. They were there to offer support to Joyce and the girls in their time of need and were huddled around a scanner tuned to the local police frequency. Rita later recalled that they had never even heard of Carmen Colon, so the thought of such an awful fate never crossed her mind when they were waiting for Wanda to return.

At 10:15 that morning, before authorities had arrived at the house bearing the bad news, Joyce heard over the scanner that a young girl's body had been located at a rest area in Webster. Chief of Detectives Andrew Sparacino said the physical features and clothing led him to believe the body found was that of Wanda Walkowicz. Collapsing under the gravity of the unthinkable news, Joyce was taken to Rochester General

Hospital and treated for shock. Fourteen hours earlier when she first called in the missing persons report, she felt hopeful that her daughter would be found safe and sound. But as dusk turned to dawn, she knew. Before the devastating news even broke over the scanner, before her family even identified Wanda's lifeless little body, Joyce knew her first child would not be coming home again.

By 10 A.M. on April 3, 1973, it was a drizzly 39 degrees— cold and damp, just like the night before. New York state trooper Thomas Zimmer was on routine patrol along NYS Route 104 in Webster when he pulled onto the approach ramp of the old Irondequoit Bay rest area just before the bridge that crosses over the bay. After a long North Country winter, anything of color stood out easily amid the browns and grays of dead foliage. That's how he spotted something white on the hillside. With the image of Carmen Colon's body beside the road still fresh in his mind, he decided to take a closer look at the white object about thirty feet downhill from the rest area. It was a little girl's bare legs. Wanda was lying facedown on the cold, barren ground, still wearing the dress she had worn to school the previous day. The search and rescue was called off; for now they had a homicide on their hands.

Dr. John Edland, the same medical examiner who performed Carmen's autopsy, determined that Wanda, too, had been sexually assaulted before being strangled to death with an object, perhaps a smooth belt. Police theorized that she may have been murdered to prevent identification of the rapist, assuming it was someone she knew. Unlike Carmen, who was left naked from the waist down, Wanda at least still had on her dress, through no mention was made of her underclothing, shoes, or socks. Some sources did say she appeared to have been re-dressed. Stomach contents revealed that Wanda had eaten custard within two hours of her death, even though she left home with no cash and had not purchased such an item at the Hillside deli. In fact, her mother later told police that Wanda would never have eaten food provided by a stranger, because she was a nervous child, and it would upset her stomach too much. Therefore, she either knew her killer well enough to gratefully accept his offer of a treat, thinking she was going to be taken home right afterward, or she accepted the food under duress, perhaps being ordered to eat something under threat of violence.

With Sparacino, Capt. Richard Boland of the New York State Police, and detective Lt. Anthony Fantigrossi of the Rochester Police Department Homicide Squad at the helm, a force of fifty officers was dispatched to canvass the Walkowicz neighborhood, as well as the location where the body was found, methodically going door to door to check if anyone had seen anything suspicious in either location. There was no such luck, even though Boland initially felt confident that the neighborhood was too populated for someone not to have seen something. While that may have been true on a nice, sunny day when everyone was out and about, the day Wanda disappeared was cold, wet, and miserable.

Two detectives from the Monroe County Sheriff's Office who had investigated the Carmen Colon murder were assigned to Wanda's case, on the chance that the two homicides were connected. After all, the girls were nearly the same age, both had been abducted while running late-afternoon errands for their mothers, and both were found by the side of a road raped and strangled to death. Webster and Irondequoit investigators scoured the Irondequoit Bay Bridge area where the body was found, while city and state investigators concentrated their efforts this time on the northeast side of the city.

Authorities spent the first few days bringing in men, including known sex offenders living in the area, who had been questioned regarding Carmen's murder. An elderly man who had offered Wanda and her friend "a dime for kisses" in a playground two years earlier was questioned, according to the *Times-Union* of April 4, 1973, as was an ex-con who had attacked a young girl in the late 1960s. Because Joyce Walkowicz had been heavily medicated since the night Wanda disappeared, investigators had to wait to interview the distraught mother until she was more coherent. In the meantime, close associates were questioned, such as a Walkowicz family friend who had played cards with Wanda for several hours the night before she disappeared. His alibi checked out.

A helicopter was dispatched, along with a police photographer, to take aerial images of both Avenue D and the east side of Irondequoit Bay in Webster. Roadblocks were set up on Conkey Avenue around 5 P.M. to see if motorists who normally drive through the area at the time of day when Wanda was last seen had noticed anything suspicious on Monday night. The license plates of individuals who seemed to be attempting to avoid the roadblocks were recorded by officers in unmarked cars, so authorities could later track them down and question them to find out what they were hiding. Yet with all the intense efforts, by day four, they still had nothing. No one saw Wanda get into a car or walk into a house or building. And the bag of groceries that may have caused all the trouble in the first place was never recovered.

Police believed that Wanda had been picked up or had gone voluntarily into the home of someone living near School 8, the last place that the other three youths walking on Conkey Avenue had seen their friend that day. Those who knew her—family, teachers, and friends—said Wanda would never have accepted a ride from a stranger, unless perhaps he was dressed like a police officer, postman, clergyman, fireman, or a woman. They said she was too street-smart. She knew better. And her playmates said she would have put up a fight if someone had tried to force her into a vehicle. Based on these assumptions, investigators considered it a strong possibility that Wanda knew her killer and had gone willingly with him. As mentioned earlier, victims of child molestation usually know their attacker very well. On the other hand, Sparacino said that some "sex perverts," such as situational-type child molesters, don't plan ahead. They have an immediate need that must be satisfied, so they strike when the need and opportunity simultaneously arise. The fact that Wanda had to walk by and was last seen at her school grounds is noteworthy, because such facilities are magnets for child sexual predators.

It is possible that a little girl carrying a single bag bursting at the seams in the rain would reluctantly accept a ride from a perfect stranger. She was only two-tenths of a mile from her house when she was last seen. Maybe she thought, what's the harm?

Four days after Wanda was abducted just minutes from home, loved ones were saying goodbye and burying her. Following a prayer service attended by about a hundred people at Ferleski's Funeral Home at 8:30 Friday morning, a funeral service was held at the colossal, gothic St. Michael's Roman Catholic church on North Clinton Avenue. A heavy rain fell over the city that morning, prompting Father Benedict Ehmann to tell *Times-Union* correspondent Judy Adams that it was like Mother Nature sympathized with the community over its loss. A small, white and gold casket adorned with a spray of white and pink flowers was wheeled into the church bearing Wanda's remains, followed immediately by Joyce and Rita, leaning on each other for support. Two hundred mourners who had come to pay their respects to the family followed them. In front of the church, two dozen young students from Wanda's school sat in sobering silence. More than a few sobs were heard when Father Ehmann said, "[Wanda] has returned to her Heavenly Father and to her earthly father. She has left her mother to go to her father." So much tragedy had befallen the family. Joyce and Rita leaned on each other as they followed the tiny casket out of the church an hour after the mass. The rain had stopped, and the funeral procession continued to Wanda's final resting place at Holy Sepulchre Cemetery, the same cemetery Carmen Colon had been buried in seventeen months earlier.

During the mass, Father Ehmann offered a prayer for the "yoke of fear" to be lifted off the neighborhood, according to the *Times-Union* of April 6, 1973. Indeed, the day after Wanda's body was found, the fear on the streets was palpable. The *Times-Union* of April 4 ran a blurb called "Colon Case

Similar," saying that police were speculating the cases might be linked. This was the first mention of the similarities between the two girls' deaths. Nobody had a clue who the killer was or if and where he would strike next. Traffic jams plagued the local elementary schools at both the beginning and end of the school day, as concerned parents of walkers decided to drive their children to and from school, watching them go safely inside and seeing them all the way safely back home. A paperboy told the *Times-Union* that at least in the Walkowicz neighborhood, and up and down Conkey, "parents were keeping their daughters indoors." Occasionally, you'd see boys on the streets; but young girls either walked in groups or with their parents.

The day after Wanda's body was found, the Gannett Rochester Newspapers once again stepped up to the plate with a reward of $2,500 for information leading to the apprehension of the killer. As was the case with Carmen Colon, a "secret witness" line was quickly implemented at which callers could identify themselves or remain anonymous. Regardless of which option they preferred, they were assigned a six-digit number, which was required to claim their reward, if one was to be forthcoming. Those who preferred sending their tips in by mail were instructed to write a six-digit number in their own writing on the upper right corner of their letter and anywhere else within the letter itself. They were to tear off and keep the number they had written in the upper right corner to provide in the event their tip proved fruitful.

A week after the secret witness program had been implemented, it received nearly four hundred phone tips and letters that were turned over to the police. The Citizens for a

Decent Community (CDC) initially offered a reward of $1,000, an amount increased to $6,000 when the Rochester Auto Dealers Association contributed $5,000 to the fund. By April 11, just a week after Wanda's murder, rewards leading to the killer's identity had climbed to $9,951—equivalent to more than $46,000 today. As with Carmen Colon, the CDC on April 25 sponsored five billboards offering a $10,000 reward for information leading to the killer. If anyone in that lower-middle-class neighborhood knew anything, they would have come forward anonymously; if not for ethical reasons, then certainly for the economic incentive.

One lead from an anonymous caller came in on the secret witness line on April 5. He claimed to have seen a man force a red-haired girl into a car at the corner of Conkey Avenue and Wanda's street between 5:30 and 6 P.M. three nights earlier. The car, he said, was a light-colored Dodge Dart. A different individual called in to say he had seen a similar car at the rest area where Wanda's body was found. Still another person reported seeing Wanda actually dumped from a similar car at that rest area. A police bulletin was then issued for all officers to be on the lookout for a light-colored, Dart-type vehicle. Unfortunately, when police appealed to the first anonymous tipster who allegedly saw Wanda enter the car on the street corner to call them back, he never did. The two related tips from other sources didn't pan out either, leaving investigators wondering why the first witness didn't call back and if what he saw was related to the case or not.

Maj. Charles Bukowski of the New York State Police told the media that there were a number of potential suspects in the homes along Conkey Avenue that Wanda passed on her way to and from the deli, and each one was being methodically checked out. Police then received word that a couple of ten-year-old girls said they had been approached the Saturday before Wanda disappeared by a man about thirty years old wearing a long, black coat who tried to get them into a 1971 Ford LTD that was black on the top and white on the bottom. The man had a black beard and a mole on his forehead, according to the *Democrat and Chronicle* of April 5, 1973. The incident took place on the other side of the Genesee River, directly west of where Wanda had disappeared.

On April 6, police questioned an Avenue D man for twelve hours. He had been charged just five months earlier with endangering the welfare of a child, and city detectives were hopeful that this would be their big break. In fact, Sparacino took down phone numbers of reporters who were following the story, in case they were able to announce the arrest of the suspect over the weekend. But the man passed a polygraph test and provided a solid alibi, so he was cleared, much to the chagrin of the authorities who admitted it had been the only viable lead up until that point.

At about the same time the previous year that the man from Avenue D was charged with endangering the welfare of a child, another murder occurred across the road from School 8 on Conkey Avenue, less than fifty feet from where Wanda was last seen alive. In that incident, José Bas, the owner of a store at 262 Conkey, was shot in the face and killed during an alleged attempted holdup. The killer was never found and there were no witnesses, so police could only speculate that burglary was the motive. But what if the reason Bas was silenced had something to do with him bearing witness to another crime? What if he was killed because he was aware of another neighborhood child being molested, for example? His stepson, Federico Mercado, took over the store after Bas's death. Mercado, like most people living or working along Conkey Avenue, said he was questioned by police at least ten times the week Wanda disappeared, but he said he didn't recall ever seeing her.

Two weeks after Wanda's murder, a gas station attendant told police he had seen a green Ford Pinto pull into the parking lot with a young girl inside who was crying and looked as though she was trying to get out. The driver was white and about forty years old. He had a tattoo on his right forearm. Other people called in regarding the same scene, so the police appealed publicly to the driver to come forward for questioning, but he never did. The identity of the girl in the car has never been determined. But police still wonder why, if the driver of that vehicle had nothing to do with the crime, had he not come forward to clear his name?

A month later, an article in the *Times-Union* called "Probe into Wanda's Slaying Could Be Nearing Dead End," said that after one of the most exhaustive murder investigations in Monroe County history, Wanda's killer still eluded law enforcement officials. Now they had two unsolved murders of preteen girls, both under remarkably similar circumstances, to consider. Two families had been devastated; two neighborhoods had been turned upside down.

Joyce Walkowicz required medication for depression for quite some time after her daughter's murder. How does a mother recover from a loss that consumes her thoughts day and night? She began chain-smoking to help take the edge off, but visions of her daughter being raped and strangled plagued her relentlessly. Joyce admitted to reporters that both she and Rita suffered nightmares, and whenever she ventured out of her apartment, she always wondered if the man walking past her was her daughter's killer. She lost twelve pounds. She lost any hope of ever getting a good night's sleep again. She lost the trust she once had in neighbors and acquaintances. Many days she felt like she had lost the will to live. And, as if things couldn't possibly get worse, three months after she lost her precious daughter, she lost her common-law companion. Raney moved out, leaving Joyce alone again to raise her two remaining daughters.

In October 1973, a month before the next young victim was slain, a program called "Eyewitness Crime" on local TV Channel 13 in Rochester resulted in roughly two hundred additional tips for police to consider in the Wanda Walkowicz murder. Fifty-five were promising enough to check out, yet not a single one of them proved useful.

MICHELLE MAENZA

Ten months after the body of Wanda Walkowicz was found in the town of Webster, eight miles northeast of the city proper, a young Webster Crescent resident disappeared as she walked home from school alone on Webster Avenue in Rochester. Like Wanda and Carmen, Michelle Maenza was on a late-afternoon errand for her mother when she was abducted. Authorities had seen the word "Webster" in police reports an awful lot that year: the town of Webster, where Wanda's body was found; Webster Avenue, where Michelle was last seen walking; and Webster Crescent, where Michelle lived. Was it yet another mere coincidence of many in the Double Initial murders, or did the killer have a subconscious affinity for the word, thus imparting an unintended clue to his connection with two of the Double Initial deaths?

Christopher and Carolyn Maenza had much to be thankful for at Thanksgiving in 1962. In a few days, their first daughter, Michelle, would be born, joining their sons, Stephen and Angelo. Years later, when Michelle's parents separated, her two brothers went to live with Christopher at 21 Hall Street in the city, and Michelle remained with her mother at 25 Webster Crescent, along with younger sisters Marie, who was eight, and baby Christine. In a *Times-Union* article dated November 27, 1973, Christopher described eleven-year-old Michelle as quiet, happy-go-lucky, and friendly, but he said his oldest daughter seemed emotionally immature compared to other girls her age. Michelle was, by all accounts, teased and picked on relentlessly by kids her own age because she was overweight. She preferred to hang around with younger children; they looked up to her and accepted her just as she was. Academically, she did fine, con-trary to misinformation that circulated over the years. School staff told the *Times-Union* in December 1973 that Michelle was an average student who fell "into the normal range . . . and is making satisfactory progress."

Carolyn was a protective mother. She always had her three daughters with her wherever she went, according to neighbors on the dead-end Webster Crescent, whether she was going to the laundry, a store, or a friend's house. Carolyn usually walked up Webster Avenue to School No. 33 each afternoon, with Christine in a stroller, to accompany her two older daughters and another neighborhood girl, even though some of Michelle's fifth-grade peers teased her about walk-ing home with her mother. They called her a baby, the neigh-bors later reported.

On November 26, when Carolyn arrived at school at dis-missal time, only eight-year-old Marie and the neighbor girl came out; they told Carolyn that eleven-year-old Michelle had to stay after. Carolyn then made a decision she would regret for the rest of her life. She walked back home with just the baby and the two younger girls, confident that Michelle, who would turn eleven the next day, would be fine walking home alone. She'd done it before without incident. Carolyn was unaware that Michelle had been having a day that was fast going from bad to worse. Statements made recently on blogs by students in Michelle's class confirmed that she had been unfairly kept for detention, along with the girl who was her tormentor that day. Between 3:05 and 3:15 P.M., Michelle finally left School 33 and headed down Webster Avenue alone.

Normally, Michelle would walk past her uncle's gas station at the intersection of Webster Avenue and Melville Street, just a few hundred feet from her doorstep. But not that day. She was on a mission to locate her mother's purse that had been left at the Super Saver store in Goodman Plaza the previous Saturday, so she turned right at Ackerman, according to two of her neighborhood friends. Debra and Sharon Ciravolo had passed Michelle as she turned the corner onto that street. She may have then walked along a short entrance road leading to the plaza, or more likely, she cut through a barren corner lot adjacent to the plaza parking lot. Police believe she may never have reached the plaza.

From where the gas station was located, Philip Maenza had a clear view of his sister-in-law and nieces walking by every morning and every afternoon. He would have been expecting Michelle a bit later that day, after seeing Carolyn walk by one daughter short. When questioned the evening his niece disappeared, Maenza said he "didn't see the girl pass," according to a *Times-Union* article of November 27, 1973, the very first article released regarding Michelle's disappearance. But in a March 1, 2009, *Democrat and Chronicle* article called "'Double Initial' Murders Remain Mystery after 35 Years," Stephen Maenza, Michelle's older brother, told staff writer Gary Craig that their Uncle Philip did, in fact, see and speak to Michelle at the plaza that afternoon and even offered her a ride home, but Michelle refused the offer. If this is true, then Philip may have been the last person who ever spoke to Michelle, aside from her killer. And that is important. Stephen speculated that the killer must have picked up his sister shortly after their uncle left her behind at the plaza. He said Philip was upset that he didn't insist Michelle go with him that day. But why did he say he "didn't see the girl" in 1973 when he was first asked? Perhaps he meant he didn't see her again after he offered her the ride that she declined, or his statement was misreported.

When Michelle hadn't returned home by 5:00 that afternoon, her distressed mother went to the house of her neighbor, according to an article on November 29, 1973, called "Shroud of Fear Descends on Neighbors of Michelle" in the *Times-Union*. The woman said Carolyn "could hardly talk," she was so worried. At 5:40, Carolyn called the Rochester Police Department to report her daughter missing. Friends and family assured the authorities that Michelle had never run away before, and Carolyn said she was unaware of any school or home issues that would have caused her oldest daughter to do so then. Abduction had become a distinct possibility. According to the director of health and physical education for the Rochester city schools, Nicholas Zona, all children in fourth through sixth grade were required to watch a movie called *Stranger Beware*. Michelle knew not to willingly get in a car or walk off with a stranger. Had she gone with someone she knew?

By now, the various agencies working together knew the drill. Another young girl was missing, and foul play was suspected. She had hazel eyes and shoulder-length, dark brown hair with bangs, and she was last seen in the vicinity of Webster Avenue and Goodman Plaza wearing a long purple coat with silver trim, black boots that went to her knees, and purple slacks with a zigzag pattern. Her description was broadcast hourly over police radios in patrol cars throughout the night. The northeast part of the city was immediately and painstakingly searched with special emphasis on Michelle's neighborhood, where a door-to-door search had commenced and continued throughout the night. When that yielded no results, police and investigators spread out, canvassing parking lots, parks, and deserted areas, all to no avail.

"A massive countywide search was launched overnight," began the *Times-Union* story on November 27. But that was precisely the problem. Authorities had no idea that the perpetrator would soon hop across the county border with his young victim, so the concentrated search efforts east of downtown that night were all for naught. Investigators checked out various reports that a girl who looked like Michelle had been spotted at the plaza entrance around 3:30, running along Parsells Avenue and Stout Street toward Webster Avenue at 4:30, and playing near Burrows Street at 5:30.

The first two scenarios, especially the sighting at the plaza entrance, were conceivable. The Burrows Street report was improbable. For one thing, it's all the way across Rochester on the other side of the Genesee River, and Michelle wouldn't have been playing along railroad tracks when she knew she was expected home two hours earlier. She was a very eager-to-please child and would never have purposely given her mother cause for concern like that. One individual told police she had seen a frightened girl who looked like Michelle in the passenger seat of a dark green pickup traveling down Brown-croft Boulevard, five minutes east of Webster Avenue, around 5:40 P.M. on the day she vanished. Indeed, there were several calls early on about girls crying in cars on the day Michelle vanished, just as there had been in the Wanda Walkowicz case. And, like the previous case, none panned out.

As dawn broke without a single productive lead, family and authorities became less optimistic that Michelle would be found alive. Carolyn Maenza, like Joyce Walkowicz and Guillonina Colon before her, collapsed and was rushed to the hospital and placed under sedation as police continued their meticulous manhunt.

At about 9:15 A.M. on November 28, two days after Michelle Maenza had last been seen alive, her badly bruised, fully clothed body was found dumped in a ditch in a rural area of Wayne County about seventeen miles east of where she had last been seen. Eugene "Gene" Van deWalle, then fire chief of the Walworth Volunteer Fire Department, told police he was driving east on Eddy Road en route to 476 Eddy Road to pick up Richard Stalker so they could look at a new fire truck together. He spotted Michelle's crumpled body in the grass by the north side of the road, seventy yards from the intersection with Mill Road in the town of Macedon, according to a *Democrat and Chronicle* article dated November 29, 1973. Van deWalle later told staff writer Bennett J. Loudon in a May 26, 2001, article that his first thought that terrible day was not to go near the body, because it could become tainted with "evidence of [himself] on her." Working in emergency services alongside law enforcement, he was certainly well aware of crime scene protocol and evidence collection. He then called the sheriff's department on the two-way portable radio in his truck and told them he needed a deputy at that location stat, having the presence of mind to omit the reason, since the public might be listening on police frequencies.

When Michelle's body was dumped, it had come to rest on its side, as if it had been tossed out of a vehicle and rolled down the side of the road into the ditch. Like Wanda, Michelle had been redressed, but several snap fasteners on her shirt had been torn in the assault, according to Fantigrossi. Michelle's coat was found in the ditch half a mile away, between where her body had been dumped and Richard Stalker's house. This means the killer probably either left the coat at the scene of the crime before dumping the body elsewhere or he noticed it still in his vehicle after disposing of the body and tossed it out the window as he drove away, the same way it appeared Carmen's had been discarded.

A woman who lived close to where the body was found told police that after her dogs woke her up around 1 A.M. on Wednesday morning barking, she thought she heard a "bang," like a vehicle's door slamming. Another local saw a slow-moving vehicle going down the road around 10:30 P.M. on Tuesday night. In that rural stretch of Eddy Road, there was rarely traffic, so people were alert to anything unusual. At any rate, because the murders had now crossed the county border, the Wayne County Sheriff's Office came on board as the lead agency in Michelle's murder investigation, working alongside the Rochester Police Department, the Monroe County Sheriff's Office, and the New York State Police, all of whom were still trying to solve the Carmen Colon and Wanda Walkowicz murder cases. Former Wayne County sheriff Richard Pisciotti recently told reporter Gary Craig that his car was the third at the scene when Michelle's body was found, and he was tasked with not only photographing that location but also the entire autopsy. He said the images he witnessed are forever seared in his memory.

The similarities between the three murders were uncanny, prompting Sparacino to confess to the press after Michelle's body was found that there was a very strong possibility that one individual had committed all three crimes. The thought of a lone predator out there on the prowl intent on finding little girls to rape and slay further heightened the paranoia in the Rochester community, especially for families who had young daughters with double initials in their names. But Fantigrossi, who was head of the physical crimes unit, stressed that such coincidences were not necessarily significant.

What interested police even more than the double initials were the striking similarities in the modus operandi, or method of operation, of the killer. He targeted prepubescent girls, abducted them from the streets in broad daylight, violated them, strangled them, and left their bodies pitilessly on the sides of roads with little attempt to conceal them. Either he didn't care whether or not they were found, or he actually wanted them to be found, because he enjoyed playing cat and mouse with the local authorities. Perhaps he enjoyed stringing them along and outwitting them with what he thought was his vast knowledge of crime scene protocol. Maybe seeing the fruits of his labor detailed in the media was somehow rewarding. Regardless of what investigators thought was "significant" or the public felt was noteworthy, the bottom line was that children were being snatched off the streets of Rochester and murdered. Rochester residents had every reason to fear for the safety of their families. How can three little girls vanish in broad daylight without anybody seeing a thing?

Michelle's body was taken to Newark State Hospital where her father Christopher Maenza, accompanied by his brother Philip, arrived at about 2:55 P.M. to identify her. Christopher left the facility in tears. When Carolyn received word that the deceased was in fact Michelle, she again had to be rushed to Genesee Hospital and placed under sedation. An autopsy was performed by Dr. William Welch, the assistant Wayne County coroner, who was assisted by Dr. Edland, the Monroe County medical examiner who had performed Carmen's and Wanda's autopsies. Edland was there to find any similarities in the manners of death. Michelle's official cause of death was "asphyxiation by strangulation," and she had been brutally raped before being murdered, like her predecessors.

It was reported in the *Democrat and Chronicle* that Michelle's body bore marks about the face, neck, and one arm. It appeared that a garroting device, perhaps a thin belt, had been used to strangle both Michelle and Wanda. Michelle's neck had a clean red line circling it, as well as bruising that indicated the killer used both his hands and an object to strangle her. In addition, bruises were found on her upper arms and elsewhere. Based on the remains of a cheeseburger found in her stomach, Edland determined that Michelle had eaten within an hour and a half of her death. She carried no money on her and had not stopped anywhere to eat between the school and where she was last seen heading toward Goodman Plaza, so when and how she had an opportunity to eat a cheeseburger is unknown. As in the case of Wanda Walkowicz, whose stomach contents revealed she had ingested a custard-like food shortly before her death, there is no evidence to explain how these girls acquired food. Carmen Colon's stomach had evidence of a corn-vegetable mixture in it, but early news reports said it was probably from something she had eaten at dinner that day before she left to run the fateful errand for her mother.

In this case, unlike the two previous ones, Dr. Edland was able to lift finger and palm prints off Michelle's neck using a new technique involving iodine and silver. Fingerprints were also discovered on a boot she was wearing, as well as on her coat. Thanks to modern forensics unavailable at the time of the murder, those prints may prove pivotal in identifying her killer today. Edland believed her death likely occurred late Monday, the evening she went missing, based on the state of early decomposition. If the body was disposed of soon after the murder, as believed, it would have been in plain sight for at least thirty-six hours before discovery.

In the two-day span between when Michelle vanished and when her body was found, she had a birthday, according to her brother Stephen. But on December 1, 1973, instead of playing with new presents or watching cartoons like she normally would have been doing on a chilly Saturday morning, Michelle Maenza was laid to rest. She never got a chance to open her presents that year. Instead, her lifeless body, clothed in a black dress and white top, was laid out in a small brown casket and buried in Holy Sepulchre Cemetery, where Wanda and Carmen's bodies had been interred. More than four hundred people paid their respects to the Maenza family at the wake at the Profetta-Nanna Funeral Home on November 30. The next morning, sixty people attended the funeral at Corpus Christi Roman Catholic Church at 864 East Main Street.

Two days later, the *Democrat and Chronicle* reported in its story "Outside a Rose Bloomed" that against the stone exterior of the front of the church, a single red rose stubbornly remained in bloom with winter fast approaching. It was like a divine message marking the saddest of occasions. The news article referenced an ancient quote by an early Christian author, Tertullian, to demonstrate that point: "If I show you a rose, you will not find fault with God." The original phrase was actually, "Rosam tibi si obtulero, non fastidies creatorem," or "If I give you a rose you will not disdain its creator."

The funeral procession continued past the red rose, and the casket bearing the grief-stricken mother's first baby girl was carried into the church by five men. With the assistance of two men at her side, Carolyn somehow managed to get through the most painful ceremony of her life.

During the funeral, police responded to a report that a mysterious car was parked in front of the church, but by the time they arrived it was no longer there. Police then monitored Michelle's burial at Holy Sepulchre following the funeral, in hopes that the killer might show up. It's been known to happen in murder cases. But the somber interment ensued without incident. Under overcast skies, in thirty-two-degree weather, a grieving family and friends said goodbye as another little girl's casket was lowered six feet below the surface of the barren, frigid ground.

The greater Rochester area was up in arms. As had been the case twice before, the Gannett Rochester Newspapers reactivated their secret witness line and offered an initial $2,500 reward. The Northeast Kiwanis Club and the Italian-American Civil Rights League then each offered an additional $1,000, and the Trott-Emerich Post of the Veterans of Foreign Wars contributed $552 to the fund, bringing the early rewards total to over $5,000. Leads from concerned residents hoping their tips would finally put an end to the insanity began to pour in. The Rochester Police Department set up a secret hotline similar to Gannett's; between the two phone systems, more than 1,500 calls were received by December 1. Many calls, if not most, were from people with various theories but with no facts to back them up. There were, however, several good leads that remain important to this day.

One witness told police she had seen a light-colored 1966 Chevy parked on the wrong side of Eddy Road around 5:30 P.M. on the day Michelle went missing, close to where the body was later found. Crough said police methodically poured over a list of such vehicles registered in the Rochester area but found no "workable leads" from it. Was that Chevy involved in the murder of Michelle Maenza, or did it simply belong to a deer hunter, since the hunting season would have just opened a week earlier? In upstate New York, cars could be found parked all over rural areas during hunting season, from dawn until dusk.

A particularly promising lead came from one of Michelle's young friends. She said that as she was on her way to another girl's house on Monday afternoon, she saw Michelle walking down Ackerman toward Goodman Plaza. When the girl left her friend's house and headed back toward Webster, she said she saw Michelle pass by, riding in the front seat of a beige car that was speeding out of Goodman Plaza toward Webster Avenue. The car nearly collided with another vehicle that was turning from Webster onto Ackerman. The witness told her mother what she had seen when she got home, but that was before Michelle had been reported missing, so neither thought much of it again until news of Michelle's murder broke several days later. Then the mother notified police. Crough said that a leading suspect in the case, Dennis Termini, had a car just like the one seen by the girl and others at the intersection that day, right down to a distinctive dent. But nobody suspected Termini until after he committed suicide a month later.

A detective who walked the distance between the point where Michelle was spotted walking on Ackerman and where she was seen in the speeding car said it seemed unlikely that Michelle ever reached the plaza, based on the time it took him to walk that distance. This contradicted an anonymous tip the police had received the day before from a person who said a cashier at Goodman Plaza told her that a woman came into the store and said she had seen a man at a laundromat a block from Michelle's home offer the girl a ride home and that she accepted. When police located the cashier, she was unable to provide the name of the woman, knowing her only by sight. The mystery lady returned to the store the following week, but when the cashier told her the police wanted to speak with her, she refused to give the cashier her name for fear of getting involved.

Police were, however, able to glean more insight into the tip provided by Michelle's schoolmate. They located the woman who was driving the car that nearly collided with the beige sedan that allegedly carried Michelle. The woman said she was turning left from Webster Avenue onto Ackerman when the beige car came barreling around the corner from Ackerman and turned left onto Webster without stopping. There were two other vehicles at the intersection at that time. Police were looking for the drivers to see if they recalled the beige sedan or its occupants. It was from these witnesses that police got their first description of a suspect. After hearing from others who saw a light-colored vehicle speeding around the corner that day, it became apparent that the killer had been intent on getting out of that neighborhood as quickly as he could with his victim.

On December 2, 1973, an anonymous woman, presumably the driver of one of the two vehicles at the intersection, called the secret witness line and began to describe the vehicle Michelle was riding in. She then became nervous that she wasn't speaking to someone directly involved in the investigation and said she wanted the secret witness number that had been assigned to her to be listed in the newspaper with an actual investigator's name for her to call directly before she would say anything else. Such was the extent of fear in the community. People who may have seen something were fearful for their lives and those of their families, so they had to decide whether it was worth the risk to come forward with information that could potentially help police solve the case.

Police agencies were not the only ones attempting to protect the city's youth from the killer. On December 5, twenty-seven community organizations sponsored a public meeting at East High School, a few blocks from where Michelle disappeared, to offer parents ideas on how to keep their children and neighborhoods safe and to brainstorm with representatives from the city school district, service organizations, and churches. On December 6, the *Times-Union* published a plea to the killer on behalf of the community called "Open Letter to Slayer: Turn Yourself In."

A week after Michelle's body was found, police had sketches of a suspect that they distributed to news media and police agencies throughout Monroe and Wayne Counties for several days. A man had come forward with information about a strange encounter he had with a man on State Route 350, the Ontario Center Road, in the town of Macedon. According to an article called "Man Wanted; Have You Seen Him?" in the *Times-Union* of December 4, a motorist recalled that on the previous Monday around dusk, the same day Michelle was abducted, he saw a beige car pulled over on the side of Route 350 near Eddy Road, less than one mile from where Michelle's body was later found. The man slowed down to offer assistance, believing that the car had a flat tire. The witness said that when he approached the idle vehicle, the man standing beside it grabbed a young "chubby" girl and stepped in front of her so she was out of view. He then moved toward the front of his car, still shielding the girl behind him, and stepped in front of the license plate, as if to block that, too, from view. The motorist said the man took a step toward him with his fist raised menacingly, at which point the motorist rolled up his window and drove off, unaware that a child had just been reported missing. This tip was significant, because while Michelle's body had been found three-quarters of a mile from that intersection, her coat was found much closer to it. Why would a guy parked on the side of a country road be concerned about concealing his license plate and preventing a good look at a child who was with him? If the man the witness approached was Michelle's killer, was he someone familiar with police procedure or just someone who had a criminal history and the presence of mind to automatically conceal his and the child's identity?

Using the information that the Route 350 witness provided, you can look at a map from that time of the intersection and, based on what is publicly known, chart the possible actions the killer took, had he in fact been the killer. Heading south on New York 350, he pulls over near Mill Road to commit his deed in a remote area at dusk. A man in a vehicle pulls up, thinking someone's car is broken down, and offers assistance; the man leaves when he is threatened. As night falls on the rural landscape, the killer turns immediately left onto Eddy Road, pulls over again, and rapes and murders the child. Leaving the victim's coat at the crime scene, the killer drives to a point just past the Mill Road intersection, pulls over on the wrong side of the road—closer to the side he wants to dispose of the body on—and heaves the child's body down into the ditch. This and countless other scenarios have gone through investigators' minds as they've tried to put the pieces together.

From the Route 350 witness and the woman involved in the near-collision with the beige car at the intersection of Webster and Ackerman Street, police learned that the suspect may have been wearing blue jeans or dark pants, a light blue quilted jacket, and a plaid shirt. The car was light-colored, like the car seen racing away from Goodman Plaza earlier that day (and also like the light-colored Dodge Dart seen three times in connection with Wanda's abduction). The suspect was said to be a slender white male, about six feet tall, perhaps a bit more. He had clear skin, a medium complexion, and dark wavy hair, which was shorter on the sides and in the back but came down to the bridge of his nose in the front. He may have swept his bangs forward to try to alter his usual appearance, especially if he was someone well-known in the Macedon or Walworth community, or his hair may have been tousled in a scuffle before any witness saw him.

An artist who worked for the Gannett Rochester Newspapers, Richard Roberts, crafted a few sketches based on witnesses' recollections of the suspect. When the sketches appeared in regional papers, they caused a wave of calls to the hotlines from people saying they knew someone who looked just like the guy in the pictures. With the influx of leads, Sparacino brought in twenty additional investigators, primarily state police officers, bringing the total number of investigators on the case to more than fifty, fifteen of whom were assigned full-time. Much time was expended chasing dead ends. One lead, however, was promising. The day after the sketch appeared in the paper, a woman called and told police she had seen a man who looked just like the one in the sketch taking a hamburger to a young girl in a car at Carrols Drive-In restaurant in the Panorama Plaza in Penfield at about 4:30 P.M. on the day Michelle vanished. This piqued everyone's interest, because the county medical examiner had reported that Michelle had eaten a cheeseburger within an hour and a half of her death. Even more important was the location.

The distance from Panorama Plaza to the spot where the Route 350 witness saw a suspicious man with a girl was minimal. The killer could have taken NY 441 east ten miles and then simply turned right onto NY 350 and driven two more miles. The woman was questioned extensively by police and asked to sift through hundreds of mug shots. She then described the man to an artist who fashioned another sketch of the man, based on her specifications. This time, a color rendering of the suspect's face was transposed over homicide detective Joseph Dominick's body, since he most closely matched the suspect's physical traits. The result was an innovative rendition of the man seen with a young girl at three separate locations: the Ackerman Street–Webster Avenue area, the Carrols Drive-In, and the roadside of Route 350 in Macedon. In all three cases, the suspect had been described similarly by witnesses.

On December 11, authorities thought they had finally gotten a break in the case. The motorist who had approached the vehicle on Route 350 called the sheriff's department earlier that week to report that he had seen the same man again, and this time he was able to get the license plate number. Deputies were dispatched to pick up the individual to whom that car was registered and bring him in for questioning. He was detained at the Wayne County Sheriff's Office in Lyons and questioned for nine hours throughout the night.

The suspect, who resided in Lyons, was in his twenties, unemployed, and divorced. He had a criminal record, although not for sex offenses. He bore "some resemblance" to the police sketch, according to the *Times-Union*, although at five feet, ten inches, he was shorter than the witnesses had indicated. He could not recall what he had been doing on the evening of November 26. Nevertheless, police searched his home with his permission but found nothing incriminating.

Throughout the night, authorities refused to answer questions from the press. Ten reporters, however, were essentially sequestered in a guarded room at the Wayne County Sheriff's Office through the night during a news blackout, as investigators from the Monroe County and Wayne County sheriff's offices, the State Police, and the Rochester Police Department, along with the Monroe County and Wayne County district attorneys, pressed on. Finally, records of long-distance phone calls that had been made from the man's house at 2:18 P.M. and 3:15 P.M. on the day Michelle disappeared revealed that he could not have been involved in her abduction. The calls, if it was true that he was the one who made them, were from Lyons to Macedon and were allegedly about a job he was interested in. Although he lived with two other relatives, they agreed that he placed the calls, which means he would not have had enough time to get from Lyons to Ackerman Street in Rochester before Michelle vanished. As a gesture of goodwill, the suspect agreed to take a polygraph test at State Police headquarters in Farmington in Ontario County. By the time they arrived at 9 A.M., however, he had become "too tired" for the test to be effective, so it was postponed until later that day, according to news accounts. He was then driven back to Lyons by deputies and released. When he ultimately did take the polygraph test later that day, he passed; so there was no further reason to consider him a suspect.

After this disheartening fiasco, Sparacino said he would prefer that newspapers not run the infamous sketch again for a while. He felt it may have been more of a hindrance than a help and that time could be better spent concentrating efforts on other leads. Others, however, still believed in the reliability of the sketches.

Meanwhile, results from forensic analysis of evidence collected at the scene of Michelle's death were starting to come in. A January 12, 1974, *Democrat and Chronicle* article stated that a report from the FBI crime laboratories in Washington, D.C., found Michelle's blood on her coat, as well as white cat fur that had been extracted from among the coat's fibers. This was an important detail, because white cat fur had also been collected as evidence from Wanda's crime scene, and light-colored fur was found on Carmen. Today, with the technology to DNA test animal fur, the cat fur from each victim could be compared to determine if it came from the same cat. This would at least help determine if there was more than one killer involved in the three murders. One theory all along had been that the girls were lured into a vehicle by a man with a white cat. But pet fur can stick to clothes and slough off on upholstery, even if an animal has never been in the vehicle. So, while the killer may have had a white cat at home or at a place he often visited, it doesn't necessarily mean that he used it to lure the girls into his vehicle.

In 1995, Pisciotti submitted more hair and fiber samples taken from Michelle's body, along with her partial palm print, to the FBI crime lab, according to the *Intelligencer Record* from December 10 that year. He would have liked to submit a semen sample, because all they could determine from microscopic studies of the semen twenty years earlier was that they were single-person rapes, but he said the semen samples "might have been destroyed."

In January 1974, a detective told the *Times-Union* that although there were still fifteen men assigned to the case full time, the investigation into the rape and murder of Michelle Maenza was "dying a slow death." His colleagues emphatically disagreed. They may not have had a viable suspect or been any closer to finding their killer than they were the day Michelle disappeared, but they still had hundreds of people left to question. Out of a list of about six hundred possible suspects, only half had been checked out and cleared at that point. Although the tips had dwindled and the hotlines had since been deactivated, investigators still had plenty of ground to cover, including investigating a firefighter named Dennis Termini, who had committed suicide after police caught him abducting and attempting to rape a teenage girl at gunpoint.

SUSPECTS

On New Year's Day 1974, less than five weeks after the murder of Michelle Maenza, a twenty-five-year-old Rochester firefighter named Dennis Termini shot himself to death with a .45-caliber automatic pistol and was cast into the spotlight as another suspect in the Double Initial investigation. He had attempted to abduct a teenage girl at gunpoint as she left a hotel that morning, but before her screams could attract any more unwanted attention, he fled on foot, brazenly searching for another young girl to satisfy his sick, urgent need. The second victim, eighteen years old, was grabbed from behind as she walked alone in a northeast neighborhood of the city. He forced her at gunpoint into a garage and told her to undress. When she got down to just her underclothing, the police arrived, thanks to a neighbor who called the police after witnessing the abduction. Seeing the flashing lights approaching, Termini once again fled on foot.

This time he found a vehicle parked in a driveway and climbed inside, locking the doors.

Sgt. Ernest Morf was on routine patrol when he responded to the call, according to the *Auburn Citizen Advertiser* of January 1, 1974. Along with patrolman Lynde Johnston, he chased Termini through several backyards and over fences, tracing his footsteps through the newly fallen snow. The tracks led the officers to a locked vehicle, and they could see that the man inside the car had a gun. So Morf called for backup from a portable radio. As they waited, Termini shot himself through the right temple, taking his own life. It was soon determined that he was the "Garage Rapist" who had eluded Rochester police for some time. They had been investigating a number of rapes in which the victims were forced into residential garages. The unsolved rapes of at least fourteen teenagers and young women occurred in this manner from 1971 through 1973, the same period in which the Double Initial murders took place. This coincidence was not lost on police. It was at this point that Termini became a suspect in the Wanda Walkowicz and Michelle Maenza rape-murders.

Termini had lived at 159 Bock Street, only a two-minute drive from where Michelle was last seen, and investigators determined that he had stalked the very neighborhoods that Carmen, Wanda, and Michelle lived in. He operated both on foot and by car and was known to have abducted at least one of his many victims and driven her to a secluded location before raping her. But there were two things about Termini's crimes that strayed from the pattern of the Double Initial murders: his fourteen victims were older, and they were left alive after they were raped. Nevertheless, plenty of other evidence still seemed to point the finger at Termini as the Double Initial killer.

Termini had been in the neighborhood that Michelle disappeared from as she was walking home. His vehicle matched the description of the one seen barreling around the corner at the intersection of Ackerman Street and Webster Avenue, right down to the color and a distinctive dent described by witnesses. There was also a map found in the car that highlighted Wayne County, which is where Michelle's body was found. And there was a firefighter uniform in the truck; this isn't unusual for someone involved in volunteer fire and rescue, but is consistent with the theory that the girls went with someone they thought they could trust. Perhaps the most suspicious clue was that white cat fur was found in Termini's vehicle. A source recently told me that there is additional evidence linking Termini to Michelle's murder, and probably Wanda's as well, because of extreme similarities, but he could not divulge that evidence.

Decades later, armed with this information, the Monroe County Sheriff's Department obtained a search warrant to exhume Dennis Termini's body for the purpose of "searching" his gravesite, casket, and remains and obtaining a DNA sample to compare to evidence found at each of the Double Initial crime scenes. On January 4, 2007, thirty-three years to the day that Termini was buried in Holy Sepulchre Cemetery, his body was disinterred from the frozen soil and taken to the medical examiner's office for recovery of tissue and bone samples. The body was reinterred the following morning in a brand-new casket, according to Crough's book. Seven weeks later, results of the DNA testing came back, indicating that

Termini was not the rapist-slayer of Wanda Walkowicz. It has yet to be determined, however, if he killed Carmen or Michelle. Although the search warrant for the exhumation was permitted based on strong circumstantial evidence connecting Termini to Michelle's murder, authorities only have semen taken from Wanda's crime scene to compare with his DNA. The semen collected at the scenes of Michelle and Carmen's deaths is no longer available, so investigators must use what physical evidence they do have, such as palm prints and cat fur, to compare to what they found on Termini and in his vehicle before they can remove him entirely as a suspect in the Double Initial murders.

There were two prime suspects in Carmen Colon's murder who were not considered prime suspects in the murders of Wanda and Michelle: Miguel Colon and James Barber. Both could be placed in the Bull's Head neighborhood at the time of Carmen's abduction and subsequent murder, both ultimately demonstrated a violent nature, and both fled the area immediately following Carmen's death. Furthermore, authorities felt that, while Wanda and Michelle's killer was likely the same person because of strong similarities at the crime scenes that they are not at liberty to disclose, there were enough differences in the Carmen Colon case to consider that perhaps hers was an isolated crime committed by an entirely different individual.

Some investigators, including retired Monroe County Sheriff Investigator Nick DaRosa, according to Crough's book, still believe adamantly that Miguel killed Carmen. Others, like Russello, believe just as vigorously that it was Barber. Some of the crucial physical evidence collected at the scene of

Carmen's murder, as well as at the subsequent two, has been lost or destroyed over the years, according to Gary Craig in a *Democrat and Chronicle* article of March 2, 2009. There are only semen samples from Wanda's case left, according to one law enforcement official, and there is nothing to compare to Miguel's DNA that could either exonerate or incriminate him.

In December 1995, the Associated Press circulated a news release indicating that police were reexamining the Double Initial murders after receiving a tip from a convicted murderer at a maximum-security prison. The inmate claimed he knew who killed the girls, or at least one of the girls. It was a relative of his who still lived in the region. Pisciotti told the Associated Press that the inmate provided police with "some interesting things" regarding one of the crime scenes that they felt warranted an investigation. Although nothing developed further from the tip, the informant was persistent in asking police to check out the relative. When he recently sent a letter to the *Democrat and Chronicle* repeating his claim of knowledge of the killer, the police responded by obtaining a voluntary saliva swab from the relative. The alleged suspect was finally cleared in early 2009 when his DNA failed to produce a match with evidence found at the crime scenes.

While authorities were scrambling to track down known sex offenders and those with criminal records to question regarding the abductions and murders of Carmen, Wanda, and Michelle, a criminal unlike any the city had ever known was in their midst.

A serial killer is an individual who kills three or more people, often with a sexual component to his crimes. He kills for pleasure, usually choosing victims of a certain age, gender, occupation, or race. Such people tend to lack empathy or a sense of right and wrong. Serial killers are often hard to stop, because they're difficult to spot. Psychiatrist Hervey Cleckley coined the phrase "mask of sanity" to describe the image that serial killers convey to the public. Ted Bundy's acquaintances described him as "charming," and his victims never hesitated when he approached them with his arm in a fake cast, asking for assistance.

Generally speaking, the average serial killer is a single, white male with average or above-average intelligence; yet they have trouble holding jobs or doing well in school. They have often had troubled childhoods and may have come from highly dysfunctional families in which they were physically, verbally, or sexually abused by family members. In response, these emerging serial killers exhibit a whole host of psychiatric problems that begin in early adolescence: bed-wetting beyond the age of twelve, fire-starting, the torture and slaughter of small animals, and interest in sado-masochistic pornography. Enter Ken Bianchi.

Kenneth Alessio Bianchi was born to a young alcoholic prostitute in Rochester on May 22, 1951. As an infant, he was adopted by Frances and Nicholas Bianchi. He was raised in Rochester and attended Holy Family Catholic School. Then his adoptive mother divulged the fact that his real mother had been a prostitute. The disclosure may have been a defining moment in Bianchi's life, as he grappled with his early impression of females, hating his mother for what she had been and hating his adoptive mother for the pain she inflicted on him. Frances later revealed that Ken had a bad temper as a child and was a compulsive liar to boot.

Right after graduating from Gates-Chili High School in June 1970, Bianchi married, but his young wife walked out on him without explanation eight months later, seeking an annulment. This may have added to his loathing of women, and it happened in the same year Carmen Colon was abducted and murdered.

Bianchi attended Monroe Community College and took courses in psychology and police science but dropped out after one semester. He then applied for a job at the Monroe County Sheriff's Office, but was rejected. The *New York Times* of April 24, 1979, said Bianchi was "repeatedly rebuffed" when he applied for police work in Rochester. He settled for the only thing he could get with a limited educational background in police work—a job as a security guard at a local jewelry store. That's when he began to steal jewelry and changed jobs repeatedly to avoid being accused of petty theft. About this same time, Bianchi wrote to a lady friend that he had killed someone. She thought he was making it up, trying to sound like a tough guy to impress her.

Two other jobs Bianchi held while still in Rochester in the early 1970s are of special interest. The first job was soda jerk. Autopsies on all three victims in the Double Initial murders revealed that they had each eaten shortly before their deaths. Police have considered that food was purchased for them by their killer. The food appeared to be from a fast-food facility. Wanda's stomach contents showed evidence of custard and Michelle had eaten a cheeseburger.

The other job was ambulance driver. One theory about the killer was that the girls went with an individual who looked harmless or official and was perhaps wearing a uniform of some type. Bianchi, as an ambulance driver (or security guard), may have been wearing one. He had no criminal record at that time, so he was flying under the radar of local law enforcement.

In late 1975, for reasons unknown, the twenty-six-year-old Bianchi packed up and left Rochester and headed for Los Angeles in his large, used, two-tone Cadillac that was dark on the bottom and white on top. This was the same color and type of car that one of the I-490 witnesses saw Carmen running from.

When Bianchi arrived in Los Angeles, his older cousin, Angelo Buono Jr., another Rochester native who had moved west with his mother at the age of five, hooked him up with a job in his automobile upholstery shop. But it was just a respectable cover. The cousins became self-proclaimed pimps, even as Bianchi sought employment with the Los Angeles Police Department (LAPD) and the Glendale Police Department.

In 1977, one of Buono's regular prostitutes left him, a transgression that got the two men so riled up they decided then and there that the women of Los Angeles needed to be put in line, starting with the wayward prostitute's best friend. Still feeling the sting of rejection by law enforcement agencies, Bianchi agreed with Buono's idea to get their female victims in their car by pretending they were police officers. Thus, beginning with Yolanda Washington on October 17, 1977, and ending with Cindy Lee Hudspeth on February 16,

1978, the duo proceeded to trick ten victims ranging in age from twelve to twenty-eight into going with them. They were then bound, brutally raped, occasionally tortured, and finally strangled to death. Before knowing that two men were involved in the crimes, police dubbed the killer the "Hillside Strangler," because the bodies were always found on hillsides above Los Angeles.

Authorities failed to realize that one of the stranglers was literally right under their nose; Bianchi had courted the LAPD in his effort to gain employment. In May 1978, after a falling out with his cousin, Bianchi moved to Bellingham, Washington, to live with his girlfriend and son. He got a job as a security guard, watching people's homes while they were away. In January 1979, the long reign of murder and mayhem finally ended when Bianchi lured two coeds from Western Washington University to a home he was guarding by asking them to housesit for he and his wife while they were away. When the girls arrived as instructed, he strangled them to death. A note on the floor of the car they had driven to the house gave police enough information to suspect and locate Bianchi, and he was arrested the next day.

In June 1979, in exchange for testifying against Buono and pleading guilty to five of the Los Angeles homicides rather than all ten—along with the two coed murders he committed alone in Bellingham—Bianchi was offered leniency in his sentencing. In October 1979, he was charged with seven counts of first-degree murder. The trial lasted from November 1981 to November 1983—coincidentally, the same span of time in which the Double Initial murders had occurred ten years earlier, from November 1971 to November 1973.

The first time a possible connection between Bianchi and the Double Initial murders was made was in August 1981 in a United Press International (UPI) news release. The article in the *Chronicle-Telegram* mentioned similarities between the murders of the Hillside Stranglers and the Double Initial killer, such as the "smooth, rope-type objects" used to strangle the victims, the fact that the victims had been raped and then sometimes dressed again, and the disposal of the bodies on hillsides in plain view. Furthermore, the article stated, Bianchi had a blood characteristic found in only twenty percent of adult males, similar to that of the perpetrator Rochester authorities were looking for.

When Buono's attorneys learned of Bianchi's possible connection to the Rochester murders, they issued an order for Bianchi to provide wrist prints to them that might link him to the Double Initial slayings. If they could prove that Bianchi had killed years earlier, after insisting that Yolanda Washington was his first victim, then they could prove that he had a history of killing alone. Such a revelation would make it easier to convince a jury that Bianchi was the lone Hillside Strangler.

When Michelle Maenza was killed, police found a partial palm-wrist print on her neck after blowing iodine vapor across it. The killer's sweaty wrist left a residue of fats and oils that trapped the vapor. A piece of metal was then pressed on the print, transferring the iodine-etched image onto it, and photographs were taken to compare to palm and wrist prints of suspects in Michelle's death. She was the only one of the girls the new forensic procedure had been used on. On September 30, 1981, Monroe County District Attorney Donald Chester submitted the two sets of prints, Bianchi's and Michelle's, to John Hinds, a fingerprint expert with the Ontario Provincial Police Forensic Lab in Toronto. By the end of January 1982, Hinds had still not made a determination. He told *Democrat and Chronicle* staff writer Gary Gerew that it was "complicated," and that he was prevented from working on it every day because of "other commitments." But at three-quarters of the way through his analysis, he had not found "anything conclusive." Although Hinds eventually reported that the prints did not match, it bears mention that wrist prints change with age, unlike fingerprints, which remain the same throughout one's life. Bianchi's wrist print at the time of the Double Initial murders may have changed quite substantially after a decade, making any negative findings questionable.

In the meantime, while the trial of Buono was still in progress, Rochester police requested a meeting with Bianchi to question him in regard to the Double Initial murders. They were denied access to the prisoner. In 1984, Sheriff Pisciotti requested hair and fiber samples be taken off Bianchi, but California authorities refused to let him have them until their case against Bianchi was settled. Pisciotti told the Associated Press that the Hillside Strangler murders were eerily similar to the Double Initial murders in that the victims had been strangled with a smooth cord, brutally sexually molested, and their bodies left beside roads and tossed down hillsides and ditches with no apparent attempt to conceal them.

Buono and Bianchi were each sentenced to life without parole. Buono died in Calipatria State Prison in California on September 21, 2002, while serving nine consecutive life sentences. Bianchi was sentenced to two life terms at Washington

State Penitentiary in Walla Walla, Washington. He spends his time crafting letters to the media and police agencies begging them to believe that he had nothing to do with the Double Initial murders.

Crough's book says Bianchi was "working and accounted for" when the abductions of Carmen, Wanda, and Michelle occurred, and he was eliminated as a suspect by "serological comparisons." Based on DNA tests of semen samples, however, Bianchi, like Termini, can only be exonerated from Wanda's murder, but not necessarily from Michelle or Carmen's.

As of early 2009, authorities told *Democrat and Chronicle* staff writer Gary Craig that they are not prepared to completely rule out Bianchi yet, because it is unclear that all three of the girls were killed by the same man. Until that time, Bianchi remains a possible, even if unlikely, suspect in Michelle's and Carmen's murders.

No Stone
Left
Unturned

The press made much ado about the perceived similarities between the murders of Carmen, Wanda, and Michelle, specifically the double initials, Roman Catholic backgrounds, poor academics, low-income neighborhoods, and loose parenting styles. In their haste to identify a specific set of traits, the media forced each victim into a mold of their own creation, whether it truly represented the girls or the circumstances accurately or not. One of the most erroneous articles written about the common themes was by *New York Times* correspondent Tom Buckley in 1973, shortly after Michelle was murdered. The article, "Three Rape-Murders Stir Rochester," started out benign enough, with mention of the double initials in each victim's name, but from there the reporter offered his opinions as fact, regardless of moral and ethical considerations, or the devastating effect his choice of words would have on the victims' already traumatized families. If nothing else, it was sensational news reporting.

The fact that all three victims had double initials in their names was first noticed by people in the Rochester area when Wanda Walkowicz's name made headlines, especially when in conjunction with Carmen Colon in the same article. By the time Michelle Maenza's body was found, it had become an obvious, chilling coincidence and ever since then has been regularly mentioned in news articles regarding the three unsolved murders. Other names for the "Double Initial" murders emphasize the letters in the girls' names. Michael Patrick Ghiglieri's *The Dark Side of Man: Tracing the Origins of Male Violence*, published in 2000, attempts to prove that Ken Bianchi murdered Carmen, Wanda, and Michelle and calls him the "Double Alphabet murderer/rapist." In 2004, Ted Schwartz wrote *The Hillside Strangler* and called the case the "Double Alphabet murders." Then in 2007, *Daily News* staff writer Helen Kennedy referred to the killer as "the notorious 'Alphabet Killer'" in an article about a man arrested for the unrelated murder of Rochester youth Michelle McMurray in 1976. A year later, a Rob Schmidt film written by Tom Malloy called *The Alphabet Killer* was released as a fictionalized portrayal of the Double Initial murders with a supernatural spin. The film, starring Timothy Hutton, was shown in only two theaters nationally and ran for just one month, grossing a mere $80,000 in its run.

Double initials are a parallel between the victims that can not in any way be disputed. However, they are not, in and of themselves, that uncommon. While information is unavailable regarding precisely how many individuals living in

Rochester in the early 1970s had double initials, one can assume it was quite a few, because Rochester was a very populated city. This may be why Double Initial investigators have, for years, repeatedly and vocally downplayed the significance of the double initials, saying only that such theories are little more than "interesting."

Just after Michelle's body was found, for example, Fantigrossi, as reported in a *Democrat and Chronicle* article of November 30, 1973, reminded the media, and thereby the public, that such coincidences were "not necessarily meaningful." He said the rape-slaying of little girls was not a crime one plans. When this type of offender gets the urge, he acts on it, without determining whether or not the victim had double initials in her name. But there are exceptions to every rule. Dr. David Barry, assistant professor of psychiatry at the University of Rochester Medical School, told the *New York Times* in December 1973 that he had never run across anything like the double-initial coincidence in medical literature or in his own experience in the mental health field. He conceded that perhaps it had been nothing more than an interesting fluke, but when taken in context with all the other similarities of the three cases, the significance of the double initials could not be dismissed.

Oddly, cases involving missing persons and homicide victims with double initials in the Greater Rochester area are not rare. For instance, on April 11, 1976, Deborah Ruggles left her seven-year-old daughter, Michelle McMurray, home alone sleeping in their second-floor apartment at 540 Jay Street in Rochester from 2 A.M. until 3 A.M. When Deborah returned home and found her child missing, she called the police.

Michelle's body was soon found in a driveway adjacent to the building. She had been raped twice and strangled to death. Michelle McMurray was a young girl from a broken home with double initials, similar to Carmen, Wanda, and Michelle, so the community was worried that the same killer had struck again. Authorities, however, thought otherwise. They knew the inside details of all four rape-murders. The Jay Street child was quite a bit younger than the Double Initial victims, and the "sexual attack [was] different," Fantigrossi later told the *Democrat and Chronicle* on October 4, 2007, without elaborating on how it was different.

James Pressler, the superintendent of the apartment building, was interviewed at the time of Michelle McMurray's murder, like countless others with any association to the child or her residence, but there was no evidence to suspect him of having killed her at the time. Thirty-one years later, with DNA testing available, new information was uncovered that made him a strong suspect. Monroe County authorities in upstate New York then contacted the Monroe County (Florida) Sheriff's Office, who followed the suspect and picked up a cigarette butt he had disposed of. The DNA matched evidence gathered at the scene in 1976, and Pressler was charged with second-degree murder. It can be assumed that his DNA did not match evidence from any of the Double Initial victims, as those crimes remain unsolved.

There have been other double initial cases in Monroe and Wayne counties, but they involved missing women, not murdered girls. Coincidentally, twenty-one years after a witness saw a man and a girl believed to be Michelle Maenza standing near a car on Route 350 in Macedon, not far from the spot where Michelle's coat was later found, the area became the scene of another crime. Sandra Sollie was thirty-eight years old and nearly seven months pregnant with her ex-husband's baby when she was last seen at a shopping plaza in Macedon around 2:30 P.M. Her car was still parked in the driveway. Nothing looked out of place inside, except that her beloved dog, Jessie, was also missing. His dog tags were later found in a trash can at a Penfield car wash. Penfield is where a woman thought she saw Michelle Maenza at a Carrol's drive-thru restaurant with her killer. When police tried to question Ralph Sollie Jr., Sandra's ex-husband, about her disappearance, he refused to cooperate or take a lie detector test and instead hired an attorney. News of Sandra's disappearance was dwarfed by the tragic disappearance of four-year-old Kali Ann Poulton on that same day. Nevertheless, Sandra Sollie's case remains open at the Wayne County Sheriff's Department, and private investigator Richard Ingraham of Henrietta, who took the case on for free, continues his search for Sandra and her abductor.

Another crime victim with double initials was Sharon Shechter, a petite brunette and young mother of three who disappeared on December 9, 2001, before her divorce became final. Her husband, against whom she had a restraining order, now has custody of their children. Sharon's vehicle was found in a Days Inn parking lot on Chili Avenue in Gates with blood on the inside, but she has never been found. The lead agency for this case is the Monroe County Sheriff's Office, Criminal Investigation Division.

Another oddity in the Double Initial murders is the persistent appearance of the number three in the case. To start, there were three murders. Then there is a pattern in the placement of the victims' first initials in the alphabet; C, M, and W are the third, thirteenth, and twenty-third letters of the alphabet, all incidentally prime numbers. But other threes emerge. Carmen disappeared from New York State Route 33 (Main Street West) and was last seen running just before Exit 3 on I-490 West. It is presumed the killer, after he foiled Carmen's escape attempt on the highway, turned off on Exit 3 and headed toward Stearns Road in Riga where he dumped her body, and possibly killed her, less than a mile from New York Route 33A, the Chili-Riga Center Road. Michelle Maenza, the last victim of the series of three, went to School 33. It may be a coincidence, but perhaps the killer possessed an peculiar obsession with threes.

Another coincidence related to the double initials that is believed to have had some significance in the murders is that the first letters in the names of the towns where the bodies were found match the first letters in the names of each victim. Wanda's body was found in the town of Webster, and Michelle's was found in Macedon. For Carmen, the killer probably turned off at the Churchville exit, but he then turned south, away from Churchville, and drove to the corner of Stearns and Griffin roads, one mile from Chili's Riga Townline Road. Thus, although Carmen was found near Churchville and Chili, her body was technically found in the town of Riga, according to Riga town clerk Kimberly Pape, who said, "The corner of Stearns and Griffin is definitely in Riga." Still, Churchville and Chili were close enough that the killer perhaps thought he actually was in a "C" town.

Aside from the patterns with initials and numbers, there has been conjecture that similarities in the girls' backgrounds may have been a motivating factor in the crimes, but often the truth in these details gets murky. One factor that was noticed was that all three Double Initial victims were Roman Catholics. In 1970, more than a third of the population of Rochester, however, was Roman Catholic. The denomination was, and still is, at least four times more prevalent than all other religions in New York State. In the gossip surrounding the murders, the notion that Carmen, Wanda, and Michelle all attended the same Catholic church spread in the community and caused concern. Such chatter has been recently exacerbated by the movie *The Alphabet Killer*, which suggested that all three girls attended mass at St. Michael's Roman Catholic Church. The storyline, in fact, was based on the theory that a priest from that parish was responsible for the three murders.

In reality, the only victim whose family attended Mass regularly was Carmen, and while staying with her grandparents, she was likely taken to Saints Peter and Paul Roman Catholic Church at 720 Main Street West, the same church at which her funeral was held, because it was less than a one-minute drive from their house. Only the funeral for Wanda Walkowicz was held at St. Michael's; the funeral for Michelle Maenza was held at Corpus Christi Roman Catholic Church at 864 East Main Street. All three victims belonged to different parishes in the sprawling, twelve-county Roman Catholic Diocese of Rochester; therefore, the fact that they were Roman Catholic, like a plurality of families in Rochester, is where the similarities in their religious backgrounds end.

Another so-called "significant connection" often repeated in the press was that the girls all resided in low-income neighborhoods. In 1970, when the first of the Double Initial murders occurred, 15.4 percent of Rochester families were single-mother households. Of that number, all but one percent lived in low-income areas. Thus, it should come as no surprise that three girls from different neighborhoods were living below the poverty level, as their mothers struggled to do their best without dependable male figures helping to support the family. Carmen's parents were separated, and her Uncle Miguel became her mother's common-law husband. Wanda's mother was widowed, but was living with boyfriend Junior Raney at the time of Wanda's disappearance. Michelle's mother was a divorcee doing her best to raise three daughters alone, while her ex-husband raised their sons. In each case, the mother was the homeowner and the head of household.

Even in the year 2000, statistics showed that nearly one in three Rochester families were single-mother households, placing them far above the average on an index of socio-economic stress prepared by the New York State Office of the State Comptroller. Thirty percent of the city's residents were living below the poverty level as recently as 2006. Again, that's nearly one in three families. So the fact that the three Double Initial victims happened to live in low-income neighborhoods where single mothers struggled to make ends meet is hardly a significant connection.

Perhaps the most inaccurate similarity previously espoused was that the girls were poor students. Ever since Buckley's 1973 *Times* piece, in which he claimed that Carmen Colon was "slightly mentally retarded" and that "there was reason to believe" Michelle Maenza was mentally challenged as well, other sources have followed suit, making the point that all three victims did poorly in school. Yet, the earliest news articles by local reporters revealed the truth of that matter. Carmen was placed in special education classes only because her first language was Spanish and she lagged behind in English; her other studies suffered because she had not mastered the language in which the subjects were taught. At the time, this was a widespread problem; a study released the same week Carmen disappeared showed that Puerto Rican students in New York City were being placed "erroneously and unjustly" in classes for students with "retarded mental development." To make matters worse, Carmen was given the standard IQ test with her classmates in English rather than in Spanish. Like other Spanish-speaking students, she had difficulty understanding the questions, resulting in a low test score. Perhaps if the test had been given in Spanish, she would have done better. But when later news articles stated that she had an IQ of only 70, they failed to explain why.

Wanda Walkowicz missed time from school frequently, yet she managed to keep up with her peers academically. She was an average student who performed above average in reading and spelling. According to her teacher, Joseph Hillmon, she was very conscientious and attentive in her studies, and she always turned in her assignments. Her math teacher, Mary Gras, agreed, according to a *Times-Union* article by Jan Barber called "Wanda's Last Hours before Abduction," saying that Wanda was a very friendly, capable, and conscientious student. Joyce Walkowicz told the press that the report card Wanda raced home from school with the day she was abducted was her best one ever and that she planned to have it framed.

Michelle Maenza was an average student as well, according to school staff who told the *Times-Union* on November 28, 1973, that Michelle was in "the normal range" and that she had been "making satisfactory progress." She hung around with kids younger than herself, but this had nothing to do with a developmental disability; it was because the younger children didn't tease her about her weight or about her mother walking her home from school like her same-age peers did. Thus, the long-held theory that Carmen, Wanda, and Michelle all did poorly in their respective schools is entirely unsupported by fact.

Another assessment of the girls' backgrounds that was not altogether accurate was that they were raised in homes with loose parenting. The media was at time ruthless in reporting this. Buckley's 1973 piece for the *New York Times* said that "there were indications of drunkenness and promiscuity" in the Walkowicz home, that Carmen Colon's grandmother was "a tired and confused woman," and that Michelle's mother "seemed to be incapable of caring properly" for her children. He went even further, saying that the Maenza girls were apparently not "required to bathe regularly," and that they were teased at school because of it.

Carmen's grandparents took her in to live with them, even at their advanced age. They took precautions to protect her from harm in the rough neighborhood by putting up a gated fence in the front yard, where she and her cousins were allowed to play. Felix often accompanied Carmen when she wanted to walk to a nearby store. The elderly Colons took

Carmen to Mass with them each Sunday and adorned her room with religious items. Her mother, Guillonina, was initially against letting Carmen walk alone to the pharmacy on November 16, 1971. She finally gave in and allowed Carmen to go, thinking she was under the watchful eye of Felix. Besides, Carmen had walked the route by herself in the past, according to investigators. In the 1970s, it was not uncommon for parents to allow their children to walk alone to corner stores in their neighborhoods. Today is a different era. Now, with extensive media coverage on abducted children and pervasive public safety warnings, parents tend to monitor their children more closely.

Joyce Walkowicz was a young widow. Although she had several boyfriends in the years after her husband passed away and she visited neighborhood bars to socialize, that in no way implies that her parenting skills were loose. It appears Joyce raised her daughters to be helpful, responsible ladies, not an easy task considering the many obstacles life had handed the family. When she sent Wanda to the store on that fateful day in 1973, she was merely granting her oldest daughter the responsibility of helping her manage the household.

Buckley's assertion made about the Maenza household is baseless. No other articles mention the bathing issue. In fact, most articles clearly contradict such statements. One neighbor, Mrs. Walter Murphy, told Michael Zeigler of the *Democrat and Chronicle* on November 28, 1973, that Carolyn Maenza always took her daughters with her wherever she went, even when it was just next door. She often drove to the school or walked the nine blocks, pushing the baby carriage, to meet her two older daughters, as well as Mrs. Murphy's daughter, to take them home. Michelle was teased because of this. As mentioned before, another neighbor told the *Times-Union* on November 29, 1973, that Carolyn was so concerned when Michelle hadn't returned home from school on time on November 26 that she was barely coherent through her sobs. She feared the worst, even when her daughter was only an hour and a half late.

Although the preceding similarities were inaccurate or blown out of proportion, there are some incontrovertible parallels in the murders that continue to confound authorities, especially the modus operandi of the killer. The girls were each abducted at about the same time of day, late in the afternoon. All three vanished in broad daylight on busy streets without a struggle. All were walking to, or returning from, a store on errands for their mother when they were abducted. All had been raped and strangled.

Carmen's was definitely the most brutal of the murders, according to Patrick Crough. In addition to manual strangulation, her skull had been fractured and her body covered with what looked like fingernail scratches. Perhaps the killer had a ring or cufflink with sharp edges that scratched the child as she struggled to break away from him.

Wanda and Michelle, it appeared, had been strangled both manually and with an object. Buckley said in the *Times* article that the red line around Michelle's neck was indicative of the use of a "garroting instrument." The wounds found on Wanda's neck appeared to be made by a similar, if not the very same, object. A garrote is a device used for the purpose

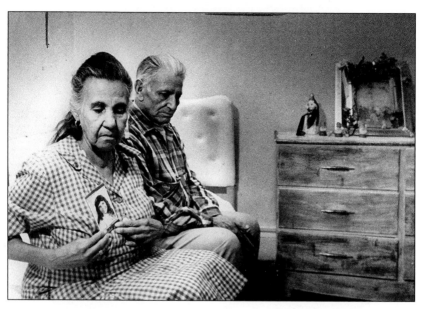

Mr. and Mrs. Felix Colon sit in the bedroom of their grand-daughter, Carmen Colon, shortly after her body was found.

Carmen Colon

Carmen Colon's body is removed from the recovery site on Stearns Road on November 18, 1971. REPRINTED WITH PERMISSION OF THE DEMOCRAT AND CHRONICLE.

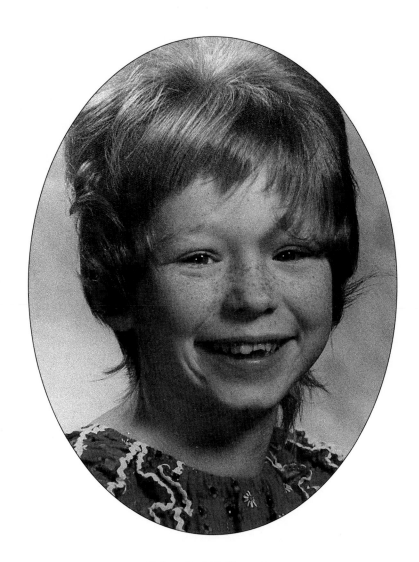

Wanda Walkowicz

Wanda Walkowicz's body is found on a hillside near Irondequoit Bay on April 3, 1973. REPRINTED WITH PERMISSION OF THE DEMOCRAT AND CHRONICLE.

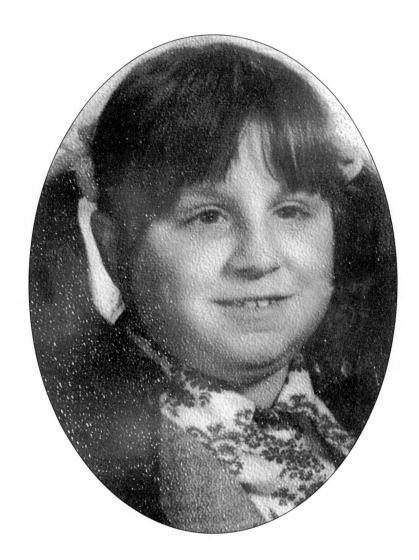

Michelle Maenza

Michelle Maenza's body is found in a ditch beside Eddy Road in Macedon on November 28, 1973. REPRINTED WITH PERMISSION OF THE DEMOCRAT AND CHRONICLE.

An artist created this image of a suspect, based on descriptions from several witnesses, by combining a facial sketch with a photograph of a similarly built and dressed man. REPRINTED WITH PERMISSION OF THE DEMOCRAT AND CHRONICLE.

of strangulation. It can be an iron band placed around someone's neck and tightened, or a makeshift wire or cord with handles at each end to accommodate the act of strangulation. It can be a catchall of any object used for that purpose, like a belt or telephone cord. The police cannot provide details of the object they believe was used in the Double Initial murders; however, the original investigators on the case said that whatever was used made them feel fairly confident that the same man killed both Wanda and Michelle.

The day Michelle's body was found, Sparacino told reporter Michael Franco in the *Daily Messenger* of November 29, 1973, that there was a "very, very strong indication" that the same man had killed all three girls. According to the *Citizen-Advertiser* of the same day, while Fantigrossi wasn't sure that Michelle was the third victim of a serial killer, he did say that the man "responsible for Wanda is responsible for [Michelle]." To this day, it seems generally accepted by officials that one man was responsible for killing at least the last two of the Double Initial victims. Many investigators continue to stop short of suggesting that Carmen's death was related. Some believe it may have planted the seed in the mind of another killer to replicate the original crime.

The last two victims were found fully clothed, which means the killer either told them to get dressed after he raped them and before he killed them or he dressed them himself before dumping their bodies. Carmen might have been found fully clothed, as well, had she not escaped running down the highway naked from the waist down. By the time her killer caught up to her on I-490 West, he was probably so intent on getting out of there, believing the cops would show up at anytime, that he didn't bother running back to find her slacks. Of particular interest to authorities at the time of the murders was the fact that the coats worn by two of the victims, Carmen and Michelle, were not found with the bodies. Instead, Carmen's coat was found in a culvert about three hundred feet from where her body was dumped and Michelle's was also found several hundred feet from her body. A couple of early news articles reported that Wanda had been wearing a red and green coat when she vanished, but all later sources said she was not wearing a coat at all when she ran what would be her final errand.

All three victims had eaten within two hours of their deaths, and Wanda and Michelle both had fast food in their stomachs. Wanda had eaten custard, though some sources said it was a milkshake, and Michelle had eaten a cheeseburger. Neither had the money or means to acquire such items for themselves between their respective homes and the locations where they were last seen. One of the witnesses in the Maenza case had seen a man carrying a burger to a vehicle with a child who looked like Michelle sitting inside at the Carrols Drive-In in the Panorama Plaza in Penfield at about 4:30 P.M. on the day she vanished. This made sense, not only because the autopsy revealed that Michelle had eaten a cheeseburger within an hour or two of her death, but also because the fast-food restaurant was right on the way to where a witness saw a peculiar man with a young girl who looked like Michelle standing beside a car near the Eddy Road intersection with State Route 350 in Macedon, less than one mile from the body recovery site. Carmen had eaten something with cornmeal in it, but authorities are still unclear on where she last ate. They believe it may have been at home before she left that day.

Cat fur was found on the clothing of all three victims. The fur collected from the first body recovery site was "light-colored"; the fur found at the other two recovery sites was white cat fur, the same type of fur allegedly found in Termini's vehicle. We know Wanda had at least one cat, because cat food was one of the items on her list at the store on the day she was abducted. While the white cat fur is noteworthy to investigators, it could not lead to the conviction of a killer at that time. With modern forensics and the ever-changing field of DNA testing, however, it can (and does) lead to convictions today.

The first time non-human DNA was used to convict a criminal was in 1994 when Royal Canadian Mounted Police detectives on Prince Edward Island found Shirley Duguay's body with a bloodied coat nearby. Two short white hairs were imbedded in the dried blood. It turned out to be cat fur. The police suspected the woman's recently paroled ex-common-law husband, Douglas Beamish, in her murder. He was living with his parents at the time and police obtained a DNA sample from his parents' cat, Snowball, and submitted it for DNA comparison with the white fur found at the murder site. It matched, linking the man to the murder of his former wife. The evidence held up in a court of law, and the man was convicted of second-degree murder and thrown back in jail. If the cat fur from each of the Double Initial murders still exists, it can be submitted for DNA analysis to determine if it came from one cat or several and if any of the cat fur matches the fur found in Termini's, or any other suspect's, vehicle.

An open case as longstanding, multifaceted, and heart-wrenching as the Double Initial murders is destined to have countless theories associated with it. The bizarre coincidences read like something out of an Agatha Christie mystery novel, making it open season for conjecture. Investigators base their theories on evidence and facts that they have gathered over the years, tweaking their theories accordingly as new information emerges and as suspect after suspect is cleared. Armchair investigators and community residents base their theories on information gleaned from the news media, online blogs, documentaries, and the gossip vine. Authors, journalists, and filmmakers rely on all of the above. Families of the victims and suspects are necessarily caught in the middle of it all, forced to relive the worst day of their lives over and over as each new lead develops and each new story appears. Carmen, Wanda, and Michelle are at peace, and several suspects have long since died, but surviving family members will always be cursed with rumors and uncertainty until every theory is either dispelled or proven.

When Carmen was abducted in 1971, police initially had no reason to believe it was more than a terrible, isolated crime. Investigators believed she willingly got into the killer's car, as all evidence suggests she hadn't been forced. Cerretto said that because nobody saw a struggle, they were led "to believe it was probably someone known to her." It is generally thought that Carmen either escaped during her killer's rape attempt or bolted after the fact, because one witness saw an unidentified man grab her by the arm and usher her back to the car, and because she was already half-naked when she fled. Her size 10 children's pants were found near the spot where she ran along the interstate, further corroborating that theory. Ceretto and Sheriff Albert Skinner agreed that it appeared Carmen had been raped and strangled elsewhere and that her body was then taken to rural Stearns Road, a few minutes from where she was seen running, and dumped in the ditch.

The Colon family wasn't so quick to agree that Carmen left with someone she knew, regardless of what the police believed. Her father, Justiniano, told the news media that his daughter was always friendly to everyone, the implication being that she probably hopped in a car with someone who didn't seem threatening, even if she didn't know them. Whether she knew her killer or not, nobody could argue that her demise was the work of a violent sexual predator, so investigators questioned all known sex offenders in the area.

As mentioned earlier, in March 1972, four months after Carmen's murder, investigators received a tip from an informant in New York City. The man told them that Miguel Colon's haste to leave the country left the tipster wondering if Miguel had something to do with Carmen's murder. Miguel told the man he had "done something wrong" in Rochester and needed to get out of town fast. A massive manhunt all the way to Puerto Rico ensued, and Miguel ultimately returned to Rochester to face intense questioning. But he never confessed to Carmen's murder and he passed a lie detector test. Although he was released, a number of investigators to this day still believe that he was responsible for the first of the Double Initial murders. They also believe that some members of the Colon family may know more than what they are admitting, based on recent comments made by other family members who wished to remain anonymous. There are, of course, members of the Colon family, including Carmen's stepsiblings, who believe Miguel was innocent, saying he was a very kind and protective father. Nevertheless, he shot at Carmen's mother and her mother's brother before taking his own life, demonstrating a tragic disregard for human life.

Another strong suspect in Carmen's death was James Barber, as discussed earlier. He was a registered sex offender, on charges from Ohio, who had been working in the Bull's Head neighborhood at the time of Carmen's disappearance. Shortly after the body was found, Barber left town, quitting his job without notice and leaving his belongings in his apartment. Although Barber is no longer living, close kin recently provided DNA samples that cleared his name.

It wasn't until nearly a year and a half later that Wanda was snatched, but the community hadn't forgotten Carmen's rape-murder. A *Times-Union* news article called "Colon Case Similar," listing the similarities in the two cases, was published just two days after Wanda disappeared, but the article did not include the double initials coincidence. Instead, the article mentioned that each girl was on a late-afternoon errand when she was last seen, they were close in age, they had been raped and strangled, and each of their bodies was found along a road. In case the two crimes were linked, two detectives who had worked on Carmen's case seventeen months earlier were quickly assigned to Wanda's case. Most investigators never see a single abduction, rape, and murder of a child. These investigators were on their second such case in a relatively short period of time. The suspects from the Colon murder were questioned regarding the Walkowicz case, and known sex offenders in the area were questioned again. Fantigrossi told the media at the time that a "pervert, a sick person is out there." He said the rape and strangulation of a little girl is not the type of crime that is planned. It's spontaneous by nature. After Michelle's murder, police were baffled as to how nobody saw two little girls being abducted off busy city streets in broad daylight. Carmen's case was puzzling enough, but now they had two girls abducted in an eerily similar manner, and Rochester residents had every reason to be fearful.

From all accounts, Wanda was street-smart. Her family and teachers insisted she knew better than to get into a car with a stranger. Friends said she would have put up a noticeable fight. But that day in the rain she was overloaded with a heavy paper bag and perhaps was willing to take the risk of accepting a ride. Those who knew her believed she would only accept a ride from a stranger if the individual looked safe and trustworthy, perhaps someone wearing a uniform like a policeman, clergyman, or fireman. Experts say molesters are rarely strangers. Sparacino told David Medina of the *Democrat and Chronicle* on April 6, 1973, that he and others in charge of the investigation believed, after listening to Wanda's family, friends, and teachers, that she must have known her killer. In later years, however, Crough said that Joyce Walkowicz became convinced that Termini, now exonerated, was responsible.

Wanda's body was found at a now-closed rest area near the bridge over Irondequoit Bay in Webster. Based on observations at the body recovery site, police have reason to believe that she was raped and strangled elsewhere. They didn't think someone would be so brazen as to commit such an act in or near a rest area for fear that they would be seen by passing traffic. But the rest area is well off the highway, and it was nearly dark out at the time of Wanda's abduction. If the urge to rape a child struck "spontaneously," as Fantigrossi put it, perhaps the killer was willing to take his chances.

Unlike Carmen, Wanda's body was found fully clothed. White cat fur was collected from her clothing and some investigators toyed with the theory that the killer used a cat to lure Wanda into his car. But the last time the kids walking a block or two ahead of Wanda saw her, she was leaning against the fence, struggling to manage the grocery bag, on Conkey Avenue; a car was approaching in the same direction that she was walking. When the children looked back a moment later, Wanda and the car were gone. Not enough time had elapsed for a stranger to pull up, roll down his window, and try to persuade Wanda to get into his vehicle using a cat as bait. She knew better. If a gun had been pointed in her face, or if she knew the driver very well, she may have climbed in without hesitation. Still, there's no evidence to indicate whether she was abducted in a vehicle or by someone on foot.

The coroner said Wanda had eaten custard shortly before she was murdered. She couldn't have bought it for herself, because she wasn't carrying any money on her when she went to the store (she charged the items she bought to her mother's account), and custard was not on the list of items she had purchased. So one would have to assume she was taken somewhere for a treat by her abductor. Would Wanda have eaten the custard if she was afraid of the person? Maybe, but it makes more sense that she was with someone she knew or trusted. Joyce said that her daughter had a very nervous stomach and couldn't possibly have eaten something under duress, and autopsy results didn't indicate that Wanda had vomited.

Another scenario may have been that an individual, stranger, or acquaintance who lived or worked in the area saw Wanda struggling under the weight of her load and approached her, as if he was coming to the rescue, offering to carry it back into his house or business for her, so he could give her a new bag. In that scenario, when Wanda stepped over the threshold of the killer's domain, he raped and strangled her there and then waited until dark to find a rest area or an area rural enough outside of the city to dump her body without being noticed.

Many believed that Wanda's was a copycat murder. Some predator got the idea to simulate Carmen's crime using the avalanche of news media surrounding Carmen's murder. Nobody was really thinking in terms of serial killers yet. And authorities were careful not to officially tie the two cases together with insufficient evidence, although there were obvious similarities. By the one-month anniversary of Wanda's murder, there were still no suspects and certainly not enough leads to keep the fifty detectives originally assigned to the case busy. News headlines memorialized the sobering sentiment, such as this one in the *Times-Union* of May 12, 1973: "Probe into Wanda's Slaying Could Be Nearing Dead End." Six months later, the case would be reenergized when another Rochester child was abducted, raped, and strangled in a nearly identical manner.

From the day Michelle was abducted on November 26, 1973, Rochester residents had the sickening feeling of déjà vu. Carolyn Maenza became so distraught when she realized her daughter was missing that she had to be rushed to the hospital and sedated, both before Michelle's body was found and after. Indeed, as one *Democrat and Chronicle* article stated, everyone feared the worst, but hoped for the best. Like Carmen and Wanda, Michelle was snatched in the late afternoon in a busy Rochester neighborhood, and nobody saw her abduction. She had been raped, murdered, and discarded over an embankment, just like the others. But only Carmen's skull had been fractured and she had human-like scratch marks covering her body. In all three cases, the killer made no attempt to conceal the body, but he did leave them in rural areas. Like Carmen, Michelle's coat was found a few hundred feet away from the body. But there were a striking number of similarities to Wanda's case that were not necessarily true in Carmen's case. Michelle was the same age as Wanda, and she had been re-dressed after her brutal rape. Her body was found fully clothed, lying face-down like Wanda's. The object used to strangle Wanda and Michelle left similar ligature markings on their necks, leading police to believe that the same object was used on both girls. Again, like Wanda, white cat fur was found on Michelle's clothing and she had eaten fast food shortly before her death.

Although a number of citizens came forward with information they hoped would help catch the killer, police never did get a big break in the case. They had a few good witnesses, like those who saw the car speeding around the corner of Ackerman onto Webster Avenue with a child in it that looked like Michelle. And there was the woman who saw a young man carrying a hamburger out to a girl who looked like Michelle in a car at the Penfield Carrol's Drive-in. There was also questioning of the man acting suspiciously near the intersection of Route 350 and Eddy on November 26, 1973. He was standing beside a young "chubby" girl that looked like Michelle near what the witness believed was a vehicle with a flat tire. That suspect passed a lie detector test, had an alibi (phone calls), and was released.

The year 1974 was ushered in with headlines like "Maenza Probe Dying," but soon all the attention was turned on Dennis Termini, a firefighter who committed suicide on January 1, 1974. Termini happened to be in the Webster Avenue area when Michelle disappeared. Investigators had reason to believe he may have been involved in at least Michelle's death. White cat fur was found in his vehicle; the vehicle itself matched witnesses' descriptions, right down to a distinctive dent. As a fireman, Termini was someone a child might trust. But in 2007, his DNA was analyzed after exhuming his remains and was tested against the semen found on Wanda, since that from the other two victims has long-since been unavailable. While the DNA comparison studies proved he did not kill Wanda, it remains to be seen if he was involved in the murders of Michelle and Carmen. If it's possible to compare Termini's palm or fingerprints to those found on Michelle's neck, or if the cat fur comparison yields positive results, he may still be implicated.

Although serial killer Kenneth Bianchi was living in Rochester between 1971 and 1973, he did not become a suspect in the Double Initial slayings until 1984, when Pisciotti heard about the Hillside Strangler in a documentary that mentioned Bianchi's Rochester roots. The similarities in the modus operandi were uncanny—rape, strangulation, leaving the bodies on hillsides—but the California victims were, for the most part, teens and older, not preadolescents like the Double Initial victims. Nevertheless, Rochester authorities pursued that lead until a palm print comparison finally cleared Bianchi in only Michelle's murder. Blood serum studies further exonerated him altogether as a suspect, according to Crough. Bianchi has been on a letter-writing campaign from his prison cell to clear his name in the Double Initial murders. He wrote recently to Gary Craig at the *Democrat and Chronicle*, saying he wanted to stress that he had nothing to do with the Rochester slayings.

The first time the media reported the double-initial coincidence was on November 29, 1973, following Michelle's murder, in articles like the *Democrat and Chronicle*'s "Killings Hauntingly Similar." It wasn't until Buckley's *New York Times* piece of December 24, 1973, that placement of the bodies in towns beginning with the respective initial of the victims was first made. He also listed the other usual similarities described earlier. It was his article, "Three Rape-Murders Stir Rochester Area," that put the slayings in the national and international spotlight, due to the broad reach and circulation of the publication.

If fears of a serial child killer hadn't crossed anyone's minds after Wanda's body was found, Michelle's murder surely got everyone wondering. Sparacino told the media that there was "a very, very strong indication" that one person was responsible for the deaths of all three girls. Fantigrossi said that Michelle's slaying was identical to Wanda's. He told the press that whoever was "responsible for Wanda [was] responsible for this." He seemed certain that the same man killed both Wanda and Michelle and added that there "was a strong possibility" that he had killed Carmen as well. If Sparacino was right, and there was one person responsible for all three murders, that meant they had a child serial killer on their hands who seemed to be shooting for every quadrant of the city. By then, the public was anticipating more double-initial murders in the months to come.

As time passed after Michelle's death, it seemed apparent that the murders had ceased, at least in the Rochester area. But the community still waited anxiously, year after year, not believing for quite some time that the killer was done with his reign of terror. Had he moved on to another city? Had he died or been imprisoned for another crime? Or is he still living in the community, smug in the knowledge that he was never pinned for the crimes he committed so long ago?

The general consensus among authorities by late 1973 was that all three girls were killed by the same individual, although there has always been some uncertainty about Carmen's slaying being connected to the other two. For example, State Police investigator Michael Iaculli said in August 1974, shortly before his retirement, that based on his intimate knowledge of the cases and of the evidence, he believed that two killers were involved. He told reporter Mike Shore of the *Times-Union* that there were a lot of perverts out there in the city, and one of them may have decided to do to Wanda and Michelle what another man had already done to Carmen. Carmen's case had captivated the entire nation for a time, because of the shocking example of crowd apathy on I-490 when the little girl was running for her life. The incident garnered massive media coverage, and sometimes all it takes is for a seed to be planted in a criminal's mind. If whoever raped and murdered Wanda and Michelle was attempting to copy the MO of Carmen's killer, he could only have done so based on the limited information made public, unless he was privy to inside facts. Such a supposition could explain why Carmen's murder was slightly different than the other two; the killer had to do his best to copycat the first crime with no more than a partial picture of investigators' findings from that first crime scene.

If, on the other hand, the killer had access to police reports or was involved in the investigation of the first or second murder in any way, or if he had the opportunity to discuss classified information regarding the case with authorities, even in a volunteer capacity, then he may have gathered enough information on the inside to replicate the first murder, making it appear that one person had been responsible for all three crimes.

Iaculli believed two killers were involved and that they lived in Rochester, because someone sick enough to do that to a young girl would not travel all the way from another city to do so. They had to know the areas of the city where they were most likely to find little girls walking alone. He told Shore that the most popular theories about how the killers convinced the girls to go with them without a struggle involved the promise of a treat or a "chance to play with . . . a kitten." Or they may have been deceived by someone who appeared to be a trustworthy authority figure. Like most of the investigators over the years, Iaculli did not pay the "double initial" theory much attention.

Without a suspect in custody, and with key evidence originally gathered at the scenes of the crimes no longer available for DNA testing, what it may boil down to is the white cat fur found on each of the victims' bodies and in one of the suspects' vehicles. It is unknown at this stage whether the cat fur was sent for actual DNA comparison. As the cases are still ongoing, investigators are unable to share that information at this time.

The theories are many and varied, but none has yet bore fruit. David Barry, the forensic psychiatrist, told the Associated Press that the killer is probably not "the obvious person", such as a registered sex offender. Police have looked carefully at church personnel, school staff, social services workers, and other similar individuals, as well as anyone who may have had access to family information about all three girls. They've left no stone unturned. Still nothing.

Investigator Crough said that Rochester authorities rely on the massive Federal Bureau of Investigation's Violent Criminal Apprehension Program (ViCAP) database and the State Police to keep their Monroe and Wayne counties sheriff's offices abreast of comparable cases. ViCap was established in

1985 to provide a national database of violent crimes, specifically murders, sexual assaults, missing persons, and unidentified victims. When agencies submit their comprehensive case information to ViCAP, detailed information goes into a national database that automatically compares it to all other cases in the system to find patterns. This would be assuming that a repeat killer hasn't changed his method of operation.

With ViCap, by disregarding the theory about double initials and looking only at the rapes and murders of young, preadolescent girls, the hits in the database increase. Any type of murder of young girls in only New York State can be selected and would result in a different set of matches. For example, on November 9, 1979, an unidentified young girl, about the same size as Michelle Maenza, was found dead of a gunshot wound to the head twenty feet from the side of the road on Route 20 in Caledonia, New York, just four miles from where Carmen Colon's body was found. Surely the proximity to the earlier crime scene, being in such a rural area, raised some eyebrows. On August 8, 1971, petite thirteen-year-old Mary Ann Wesolowski of Glens Falls, New York, vanished on her way to meet friends. She has never been found, so it is unknown whether she was abducted, raped, and strangled like the Double Initial victims or is still alive. But the fact that a thirteen-year-old child went missing in New York State just three months before Carmen Colon was abducted makes it at least worthy of comparison.

In May 1973, one month after Wanda Walkowicz was abducted and murdered, there was another ruthless child predator on the loose in upstate New York, raping and murdering children. Robert Garrow was released from prison in

1968, after serving seven years for raping a teenage girl. In 1972, he was again arrested in Syracuse, New York, on drug violations and charges of unlawful imprisonment; he had tied up two female college students, but the girls refused to press charges. In May 1973, Garrow abducted two little girls in the village of Geddes, just an hour and nineteen minutes east of Rochester. They were ten and eleven years old. He took them to a "hilly area" in Camillus, according to his testimony in court, and raped and sodomized them. He was arrested but managed to get released on bail. When he didn't show up for the scheduled court date, he became a dangerous fugitive.

In July 1973, just three months after Wanda had been raped and murdered, Garrow abducted sixteen-year-old Alicia Hauck as she walked home from high school in Syracuse, an hour and a half east of Rochester. Garrow told the court that he raped Hauck "on a hill" and then stabbed her to death when she attempted to escape. He then found a young couple at their campsite in the Adirondacks and tied the young man, Daniel Porter, to a tree before stabbing him to death and kidnapping his girlfriend, Susan Petz. Petz was sexually assaulted for four days until she tried to escape, and then Garrow stabbed her to death, just as he had the Hauck girl, dumping her body down the airshaft of a mine. He was eventually tracked down by a conservation officer who shot him in the foot, partially paralyzing him. A jury rejected his plea of not guilty by reason of insanity and found him guilty of murder in the first degree. Garrow was sentenced to twenty-five years to life in prison but was shot and killed by prison guards on September 8, 1978, after he escaped jail with a smuggled gun and shot at them.

This was a man who admittedly raped and murdered girls the same age as Carmen, Wanda, and Michelle, and he committed his crimes on a hillside less than two hours from Rochester the same year Wanda and Michelle were found dead.

There were similar child abduction murders occurring in other northern states, as well, in the 1970s. A perpetrator called "The Babysitter" terrorized Oakland County in Michigan in 1976 and 1977, abducting and murdering four children whose violated bodies had been bathed and re-dressed before being left in ditches and snowbanks at various locations in the area. Twelve-year-old Mark Stebbins was last seen leaving an American Legion hall on a Sunday afternoon in February 1976. His body, fully clothed, was later found laid out neatly in a snowbank. He had been sexually assaulted with an object and strangled, and there was no attempt to conceal his body. Jill Robinson was only twelve years old when she was snatched off Main Street in Royal Oak in December 1976. Her body was found four days later, the day after Christmas, on the side of Interstate 75. She, too, was fully clothed and had been killed by a single shotgun blast to the face. Her body, like that of Mark Stebbins, was carefully laid out in the snow. Kristine Mihelich was only ten years old when she was last seen in the town of Berkley leaving a convenience store holding a magazine on January 2, 1977. Her fully clothed body was discovered nineteen days later on the side of a rural road in Franklin Village, placed neatly in the snow. She had been smothered to death.

The last victim of the Babysitter was eleven-year-old Timothy King. He was last seen leaving a drugstore, where he had purchased candy, on March 16, 1977. Six days later, his violated body was found in a shallow ditch in the town of Livonia. Like Mark Stebbins, he had been sexually assaulted with an object and like Kristine Mihelich, he was suffocated. His clothing had been cleaned and ironed and he had been bathed. His last meal had been fried chicken, his favorite. Like Michelle Maenza, Timothy was fed fast food shortly before death, and his body was found just over the county line in Wayne County, Michigan. Oddly, Michelle's body had been found in a New York State county of the same name, Wayne, just over the Monroe County line. None of the Babysitter Murders has ever been solved. The killer's ever-changing MO made predicting his next move and capturing him exceedingly difficult.

A string of unsolved disappearances and murders of young girls in Connecticut in the late 1960s and 1970s may have had something to do with a child pornography ring in the Tolland area at the time. Tolland was the hardest-hit county in Connecticut for this series of crimes. It began in May 1969, when Diane Toney, 11, disappeared while watching a parade near her home in New Haven. She was found beaten to death with a rock, and her body had been dumped in a wooded area. On May 27 of the same year, Mary Mount, 10, disappeared while chasing her kitten near her home in New Canaan. She was last seen talking to a white male with a white car. Her bludgeoned body was found propped up against a rock in a wooded area. On May 30, Dawn Cave, 14, vanished shortly after walking out of her house in Bethany. She was found beaten to death with a rock, and her body was disposed of in a wooded area. More than a year later, in

September 1970, Jennifer Noon, 5, vanished while walking home from school in New Haven at lunchtime. Her battered body was found a few days later. Four of these victims disappeared in the late afternoon. Three of the bodies were found in rural areas within a sixty-mile radius of each other.

The killing spree in Connecticut stopped for four years, from September 1970 until November 1974, roughly the same period of the Double Initial murders in Rochester, although seven-year-old Janice Pockett disappeared from near her home in Tolland on July 26, 1973, and was never found. It seems unlikely, however, that the Connecticut child killer was the same man who killed the Rochester youths, unless he entirely changed his modus operandi from bludgeoning his victims with rocks to strangulation.

The Connecticut crimes resumed sporadically beginning on November 1974, when Lisa Joy White, 13, went missing from Vernon while walking back home from a friend's house; she has never been found. On July 21, 1975, Stephanie Olisky, 15, was abducted in East Windsor and was found in critical condition, unable to provide information; she later died. On June 1977, Renee Freer, 8, was abducted while walking to a friend's house around 6 P.M. Shortly after 10 P.M. that evening, her body was found three hundred yards from her house; her skull had been crushed.

Although the Connecticut slayings were quite different than the Double Initial murders, it is worth noting that the Rochester murders took place when Connecticut experienced a break in their child abductions and murders. Serial killers have been known to change their modus operandi, tweaking and improving it as they become more experienced, or changing it to purposely throw off the authorities.

Today, the New York State Police, Rochester Police Department, Monroe County Sheriff's Office, and the Wayne County Sheriff's Office all share information they receive regarding the Double Initial murders. They meet regularly to share new leads and ideas, and they meet with retired investigators who worked on the case through the years to glean additional insight. Like State Police investigator Tom Crowley told Gary Craig of the *Democrat and Chronicle*, investigators feel as though they are still making progress, and the thought of someday solving the cases is what keeps them going. Former Wayne County sheriff Pisciotti seemed to agree, saying one little thing may be all it takes to break the case wide open.

Acknowledgments

The person who deserves the most thanks, hands down, in this project is my husband, Leland, who helped in so many ways as I researched and wrote this book. He accompanied me to Rochester to retrace the final steps of the killer at each location where the victims' bodies were found—a heart-wrenching but necessary part of the research that brought it all home to both of us. He sat beside me, listened with great interest, and took on additional responsibilities on the home front when my weekend and late-evening hours were monopolized by research for this book.

Daughters are precious gifts. I'd like to thank my own girls for accepting why this book was so important to me to write—why I needed to do my part to keep this particular story alive. Although they would have preferred I write about something less disturbing and more resolved, it was because of my own daughters that the case grabbed my attention in the first place. They were the impetus. And I thank my lucky stars every day for them.

I can never thank my parents, Tom and Jean Dishaw, enough for their support and for providing me and my siblings—Christina Walker, Cindy Barry, and Tom Dishaw—with an idyllic, safe, and wonderful childhood. Shout-outs also go to other members of my extended family: Ed, Rachel, and

Ryan Barry; Danon Hargadin; Bryan, Lindsey, and little Cade Alexander Walker; and Heather and Amanda Walker; and my in-laws, Carol and Lee Farnsworth.

Many thanks to Stackpole Books and my editor Kyle Weaver for giving me the opportunity to change genres and for understanding my desire to do so. I also thank assistant editor Brett Keener for righting my wrongs and making me look presentable on paper.

An individual for whom I developed the utmost respect in this endeavor was retired Monroe County Sheriff investigator Patrick Crough, the lead investigator on the Double Initial case. I can't even begin to fathom the things he has seen, the situations he has walked into, and the criminal minds he has prodded for information. How does one sit across the table from someone with no conscience or remorse? I thank Patrick profoundly for his willingness to meet with me in Rochester and patiently answer those questions he was at liberty to discuss, so long as they didn't compromise the investigation. I commend him for his efforts to protect our youth. As I mentioned earlier, Patrick wrote *The Serpents among Us*, to teach people how to identify child sexual predators and prevent our children from becoming their next victims, and he founded Millstone Justice, a child advocacy non-profit organization, for the same purpose.

Many thanks to my good friend Belle Salisbury, who offered her unique insights and support throughout this difficult process.

Thanks to reporter Gary Craig for his kind offer of assistance and for keeping the Double Initial story alive in the *Democrat and Chronicle*. Jim Fogler and Dennis Floss of the

Democrat and Chronicle were very helpful in accommodating our photo requests. Many thanks also to the kind stranger standing at the proverbial fork in the road at Griffin and Stearns, for showing me which way to go, both metaphorically and literally.

Countless men have worked on the Double Initial murders since November 1971 when Carmen became the first known victim. Many were then, and are now, fathers of young girls whom it affected on a more personal level. All were determined to find the killer or killers in their time in law enforcement, even as each individual inevitably inched closer to retirement, when it was time to pass the torch to a new generation of investigators.

The families of the victims and the citizens of the community of Rochester can rest assured that no stone has been left unturned in the decades-long investigation, and never have authorities given up on efforts to find the killer, nor will they. In order to acknowledge every individual I possibly could who has ever been involved in the case, I went through all of the news articles and other sources I had at my disposal, highlighting each name. Some of the following people are now deceased, many have retired, and many have been promoted or changed jobs and titles. Following is an alphabetical listing of their names: Billy Barnes, Monroe County Director of Mental Health Dr. David Barry, State Police Captain Richard Boland, State Police Major Charles Bukowski, Lenny Burriello, Wayne County Sheriff's Department Chief Deputy Paul Byork, Wayne County Sheriff's Investigator Harry Carr, Monroe County Sheriff's Detective Chief Michael Cerretto, Rochester Police detective Tony Cerretto, the late Monroe

County Sheriff's Detective Sergeant Donald Clark, New York State Police Investigator Thomas Crowley, Vito D'Ambrosia, Monroe County Sheriff's Detective Nicholas DaRosa, Monroe County Medical Examiner Dr. Caroline Dignan, New York State Police Investigator Al Dombrowski, Homicide Detective Joseph Dominick, Monroe County Medical Examiner John Edland, Chief of Detectives Anthony Fantigrossi, State Police Lieutenant James Foody, Detective Joseph Gangemi, SUNY Buffalo Social Psychologist Dr. Victor Harris, Wayne County Detective Lieutenant Robert Hetzke, retired New York State Police detective Ed Hooper, State Police Investigator Michael Iaculli, Rochester police Captain Lynde Johnston, Wayne County Sheriff Richard Kise, District Attorney Jack B. Lazarus, Sheriff William Lombard, State Police Senior Investigator Edward Longhany, Chairman of the Citizens for a Decent Community Michael Macaluso, Chief of Detectives William Mahoney, Monroe County Undersheriff Andrews Maloney, Rochester Police Sergeant Mark Mariano, Detective Joseph Perticone, Wayne County Sheriff Richard Pisciotti, Monroe County District Attorney Howard Relin, artist Richard Roberts, Rochester Police Department's Louis J. Rotunno, Monroe County Sheriff's Detective Robert Russello, Sal Ruvio, State Police Senior Investigator John Schermerhorn, District Attorney Stephen Sirkin, Monroe County Sheriff Albert W. Skinner, Chief of Detectives Andrew Sparacino, Technician Sergeant Robert Tacito, Lou "Bopper" Tacito, Rochester Police Department Detective John Vadas, Walworth Volunteer Fire Department Fire Chief Eugene VanDeWalle, Investigator Tom Vasile, Wayne County Sheriff's Office Assistant Wayne Country, Coroner Dr. William Welch, Monroe County Sheriff's

Acknowledgments

Deputy William Yotter, Chief Investigator of the Monroe County Medical Examiner Robert Zerby, and State Trooper Thomas Zimmer.

My heartfelt condolences go to the families of the victims. I hope this book catches the eye of someone courageous enough to come forward now with information they were previously hesitant to share with authorities, so the killer or killers can be found and brought to justice, and the families can finally have some closure.

Bibliography

BOOKS AND GOVERNMENT DOCUMENTS

Brown, Katherine M., et al. *Case Management for Missing Children Homicide Investigation.* Washington, DC: Rob McKenna, Attorney General of Washington and U.S. Department of Justice Office of Juvenile Justice and Delinquency Prevention, 2006.

Christie, Agatha. *The A.B.C. Murders.* New York: Dodd Mead, 1936.

Crough, Patrick. *The Serpents Among Us.* Rochester, NY: Millstone Justice Children's Advocacy Organization, 2009.

Dworetzky, J. P. *Introduction to Child Development.* St. Paul, MN: West Publishing, 1981.

Lanning, Kenneth V. *Child Molesters: A Behavioral Analysis for Law-Enforcement Officers Investigating the Sexual Exploitation of Children by Acquaintance Molesters.* 4th ed. Washington, DC: National Center for Missing and Exploited Children, 2001.

New York State Office of the State Comptroller. *Local Government Issues in Focus* Vol. 1, no. 1. Albany, NY: Division of Local Government Service and Economic Development, 2004.

Schwarz, Ted. *The Hillside Strangler.* Sanger, CA: Quill Driver Books/Word Dancer Press, 2004.

Sedlak, Andrea J., et al. *National Estimates of Missing Children: An Overview.* Washington, DC: U.S. Department of Commerce Office of Justice Program, 2002.

U.S. Department of Commerce. *1970 Census of Population Supplementary Report: Low-Income Neighborhoods in Large Cities: 1970.* Washington, DC: U.S. Department of Commerce, 1974.

NEWSPAPER AND PERIODICAL ARTICLES
(In chronological order)

"In Memory of Little Hattie." *Plattsburgh Sentinel,* February 22, 1884.

"Missing Conn. Girl Found Dead." *Press* (Binghamton, NY), June 18, 1969.

"Police Officials Plan Conference on Three Murders." *Wilton Bulletin,* October 8, 1969.

Cooper, Dick. "Police Hunt Girl's Slayer." *Times-Union* (Rochester, NY), November 19, 1971.

"NY State News Briefs." *Citizen Advertiser* (Auburn, NY), November 19, 1971.

Ryan, Tom. "Nobody Stopped to Save Carmen." *Democrat and Chronicle* (Rochester, NY), November 20, 1971.

"Can You Help Find a Killer?" *Democrat and Chronicle,* November 21, 1971.

"Apathy Abounds as Motorists Ignore Girl, Later Raped, Slain." *Star-News* (Pasadena), November 22, 1971.

"Rewards Set for Data on Slaying." *Daily Press* (Utica, NY), November 22, 1971.

"Papers Offer Reward in Girl's Death." *Observer-Dispatch* (Utica, NY), November 22, 1971.

"More 'Clues' to a Killer's Car." *Democrat and Chronicle,* November 22, 1971.

"Funeral Held for Slain Girl." *Times-Union,* November 22, 1971.

"Study Assails Public Schools on Education of Puerto Ricans." *Citizen-Advertiser,* November 22, 1971.

Bibliography

"Girl is Slain After Motorists Ignore Her Pleading for Help." *Watertown Daily Times*, November 22, 1971.

"Search Intensified for Killer." *News-Herald* (Panama City, FL), November 23, 1971.

DeForest, Ben. "Only Death Answered Child's Plea." *Observer-Dispatch*, November 23, 1971.

"Police Report No Clues as Carmen, 10, is Buried." *Democrat and Chronicle*, November 23, 1971.

Cooper, Dick. "Did Carmen Know Slayer?" *Times-Union*, November 24, 1971.

"'Witness Line' Gets 8 Calls." *Democrat and Chronicle*, November 24, 1971.

Flickner, Sandy. "Silent Fear Invades Brown Street." *Democrat and Chronicle*, November 25, 1971.

"Hunt for Slayer Still On." *Democrat and Chronicle*, November 26, 1971.

"Girl's Slayer Still Sought." *Times-Union*, November 27, 1971.

"200 Questioned in Girl's Slaying." *Democrat and Chronicle*, November 27, 1971.

Starr, Mark. "A Day Like Every Other . . . Almost." *Democrat and Chronicle*, November 28, 1971.

DeForest, Ben. "No One Stopped!" *Lowell Sunday Sun*, November 28, 1971.

"Hundreds Saw Carmen, No Motorist Stopped." *Citizen-Advertiser*, November 29, 1971.

"Bull's Head Key to Slaying?" *Democrat and Chronicle*, November 29, 1971.

"Search Finds Slacks Worn by Slain Girl." *Observer-Dispatch*, November 30, 1971.

"Girl on X-Way 'Definitely' Was Carmen." *Times-Union*, November 30, 1971.

Akeman, Thom. "Carmen's Slacks Found in Riga." *Democrat and Chronicle*, November 30, 1971.

"Slain Child's Slacks Found." *Palladium Times*, November 30, 1971.

"Witness Line Gets 17 Calls and 2 Letters." *Democrat and Chronicle*, December 1, 1971.

Hansen, Linda. "Carmen Could Have Been Me, but . . . " *Times-Union*, December 2, 1971.

"3 Sheriff's Detectives Given Carmen's Case." *Democrat and Chronicle*, December 21, 1971.

"Slaying Clues Laid to Signs." *Democrat and Chronicle*, February 25, 1972.

"Billboards Trigger 10 Tips." *Times-Union*, February 26, 1972.

Ryan, Tom. "Billboards Seek Killer of Carmen." *Democrat and Chronicle*, February 23, 1972.

"Billboard Erected as Grim Reminder." *Amsterdam Recorder*, February 23, 1972.

Ryan, Tom. "Slaying in the Spotlight." *Democrat and Chronicle*, March 2, 1972.

Cooper, Dick, and Jim Sykes. "Hunt for Murderer of Colon Girl Shifts to Puerto Rico." *Times-Union*, March 16, 1972.

Ryan, Tom. "Hunt for Carmen's Killer Goes to P.R." *Democrat and Chronicle*, March 16, 1972.

"San Juan Tip Pursued." *Times-Union*, March 17, 1972.

"'Secret' Colon Quiz in P.R." *Democrat and Chronicle*, March 17, 1972.

"Carmen Colon Slaying Lead Found." *San Antonio Express*, March 18, 1972.

"Police Check Puerto Rico for Suspect." *Citizen-Advertiser*, March 18, 1972.

"Police Still Seek Suspect." *Democrat and Chronicle*, March 19, 1972.

Sykes, Jim. "Carmen Colon Case Stalls in San Juan." *Times-Union*, March 20, 1972.

Cooper, Dick. "San Juan Suspect Hunt Fails." *Times-Union*, March 21, 1972.

Ryan, Tom. "Arrest Near in Slaying?" *Democrat and Chronicle*, March 21, 1972.

"Slaying Suspect Search Futile." *Democrat and Chronicle*, March 22, 1972.

Cooper, Dick, and Jim Sykes. "We Were Just a Few Steps Behind the Guy." *Times-Union*, March 22, 1972.

"Lazarus Blames Press in Colon Case." *Democrat and Chronicle*, March 23, 1972.

Cooper, Dick, and Jim Sykes. "Lazarus, FBI Differ on Puerto Rico." *Times-Union*, March 23, 1972.

"Publicity Spoiled Manhunt." *Daily Messenger* (Canandaigua, NY), March 23, 1972.

"Suspect Flees; DA Cites Story." *Citizen-Advertiser*, March 23, 1972.

Cooper, Dick. "Man Returns to City for Colon Case Quiz." *Times-Union*, March 28, 1972.

Ryan, Tom. "'Hunted Man' Surrenders in Carmen Slaying Case." *Democrat and Chronicle*, March 28, 1972.

"Carmen's Slayer Under Arrest?" *Salina Journal*, March 28, 1972.

"Slaying Suspect is Held." *Daily Messenger*, March 28, 1972.

"Release Suspect in Slaying Case." *Palladium-Times*, March 29, 1972.

"Man Cleared in Colon Quiz, Heads Back for Puerto Rico." *Times-Union*, March 29, 1972.

Ryan, Tom. "Carmen Slaying 'Suspect' Cleared." *Democrat and Chronicle*, March 29, 1972.

"Suspect Not Girl's Slayer." *Syracuse Herald-Journal*, March 29, 1972.

"Leads Fading in Colon Case." *Democrat and Chronicle,* March 31, 1972.

"DA Action Unauthorized." *Democrat and Chronicle,* April 6, 1972.

"DA Defines His Duties." *Democrat and Chronicle,* April 7, 1972.

Cooper, Dick. "Thousands of 'Clues' in Carmen Colon File." *Times-Union,* April 20, 1972.

"Carmen Colon Murder: The Search Bogs Down." *Times-Union,* June 1, 1972.

Marsh, Jack, and Terry Dillman. "Girl's Body Found in Webster—May Be Missing City Pupil, 11, Police Say." *Times-Union,* April 3, 1973.

Barber, Jan. "Wanda's Last Hours before Abduction." *Times-Union,* April 4, 1973.

"Missing Rochester Child Slain." *Syracuse Post-Standard,* April 4, 1973.

Marsh, Jack, and Dick Cooper. "Search on for Wanda's Killer." *Times-Union,* April 4, 1973.

"$2,500 Reward." *Times-Union,* April 4, 1973.

"Can You Help Find a Killer?" *Times-Union,* April 4, 1973.

O'Brien, Bill. "The Little Redhead of Avenue D." *Democrat and Chronicle,* April 4, 1973.

Medina, David. "Wanda's Killer Still at Large, Police Stumped in Wide Search." *Democrat and Chronicle,* April 5, 1973.

Marsh, Jack. "Few Children on Streets in Neighborhood of Fear." *Times-Union,* April 5, 1973.

Cooper, Dick, and Jack Marsh. "Police Want Wanda Tipster to Call Again." *Times-Union,* April 5, 1973.

"Secret Witness." *Democrat and Chronicle,* April 5, 1973.

Adams, Judy. "200 Mourners Attend Funeral for Slain Girl." *Times-Union,* April 6, 1973.

Medina, David. "Leads but No Clues in Killing." *Democrat and Chronicle,* April 6, 1973.

Medina, David. "Search for Killer 'Looks Brighter.'" *Democrat and Chronicle*, April 7, 1973.

"Man Quizzed 12 Hours About Wanda, Cleared." *Times-Union*, April 7, 1973.

Musto, Paula. "Murder Lead Falls Through." *Democrat and Chronicle*, April 8, 1973.

Freadhoff, Chuck. "'Best' Report Card Will Be Framed." *Democrat and Chronicle*, April 9, 1973.

Marsh, Jack. "No Prime Suspects in Wanda's Slaying." *Times-Union*, April 9, 1973.

Medina, David. "Wanda's Neighborhood Nervous Since Murder." *Democrat and Chronicle*, April 9, 1973.

"Avoiders of Roadblocks Checked in Girl Slaying." *Times-Union*, April 10, 1973.

"Reward Funds Grow." *Times-Union*, April 10, 1973.

"No Progress in Hunt for Killer." *Democrat and Chronicle*, April 10, 1973.

"349 Tips Received." *Democrat and Chronicle*, April 10, 1973.

"Wanda Fund at $9,591." *Democrat and Chronicle*, April 11, 1973.

"Time Dims Prospects of Finding Slayer." *Times-Union*, April 11, 1973.

Hall, Dan. "Poems by Pupils in Wanda's Class Will Aid Family." *Times-Union*, April 17, 1973.

"Police Press Car Hunt in Slaying Case." *Times-Union*, April 19, 1973.

"Billboard Ads Planned in Rapist-Slayer Hunt." *New York Times*, April 26, 1973.

Marsh, Jack. "Probe into Wanda's Slaying Could Be Nearing Dead End." *Times-Union*, May 12, 1973.

Marsh, Jack. "Nightmare Haunts Her." *Times-Union*, July 16, 1973.

Musto, Paula. "Wanda's Mother Cannot Forget . . ." *Democrat and Chronicle*, July 16, 1973.

"200 Tips from TV Show." *Democrat and Chronicle*, October 24, 1973.

Marsh, Jack. "Police Hunt for Missing City Girl, 11." *Times-Union*, November 27, 1973.

Marsh, Jack. "'No Decent Leads' Yet on Missing Girl, 11." *Times-Union*, November 28, 1973.

Zeigler, Michael. "Neighbors Fear Worst, Hope for the Best." *Democrat and Chronicle*, November 28, 1973.

"Girl's Body Found in Wayne County." *Times-Union*, November 28, 1973.

Franco, Michael R. "Parents Unnerved by Girl's Murder." *Daily Messenger*, November 29, 1973.

"Police Find Body of Missing Girl; Murder Linked to Earlier Killings." *Citizen-Advertiser*, November 29, 1973.

Goldberg, Gerald, and John McGinnis. "No Leads in Slaying of Girl, 11." *Democrat and Chronicle*, November 29, 1973.

Minzesheimer, Bob. "Killings Hauntingly Similar." *Democrat and Chronicle*, November 29, 1973.

Cooper, Dick. "Shroud of Fear Descends on Neighbors of Michelle." *Times-Union*, November 29, 1973.

Pikrone, Mary Anne. "Quiz Your Child on 'Officer Friendly' Rules." *Times-Union*, November 30, 1973.

"Reward Fund Set at $2,500 by Papers." *Times-Union*, November 30, 1973.

Goldberg, Gerald. "Police Discount Slaying Coincidences." *Democrat and Chronicle*, November 30, 1973.

"Reward Offered in Rochester Child Murder." *Citizen-Advertiser*, November 30, 1973.

Goldberg, Gerald. "New Clues Checked in Slaying." *Democrat and Chronicle*, December 1, 1973.

"Muted Rage at Wake: Michelle's Funeral Held." *Times-Union*, December 1, 1973.

"Police Press Their Hunt for Rochester Rapist-Killer." *Observer Dispatch*, December 1, 1973.

"Police Watch Girl's Burial." *Times-Union*, December 1, 1973.

"Reward Fund Grows to $4,500 in Girl's Death." *Democrat and Chronicle*, December 1, 1973.

"Was it Michelle in Speeding Car?" *Democrat and Chronicle*, December 2, 1973.

"Witness Line Calls Decrease." *Democrat and Chronicle*, December 2, 1973.

"Police Get Michelle Half-Clue." *Democrat and Chronicle*, December 3, 1973.

Connolly, Tom. "Tell the Police, Let Them Decide." *Democrat and Chronicle*, December 3, 1973.

"Phone Tips 'Moderate.'" *Democrat and Chronicle*, December 3, 1973.

"Killer Arrest Reward Fund Tops $5,000." *Times-Union*, December 3, 1973.

Marsh, Jack. "Police Quiz Witness Who 'Saw' Michelle." *Times-Union*, December 3, 1973.

"Outside a Rose Bloomed." *Democrat and Chronicle*, December 3, 1973.

Marsh, Jack. "Man Wanted; Have You Seen Him?" *Times-Union*, December 4, 1973.

"Police Have Lead in Rochester Case." *Citizen-Advertiser*, December 4, 1973.

"Police Informant Describes Possible Suspect in Killings." *Palladium Times*, December 4, 1973.

"Secret 'Hot Line' Filled with Calls." *Democrat and Chronicle*, December 4, 1973.

"Scores Call in Slaying." *Times-Union*, December 4, 1973.

"Have Description of Man Sought in Death of Girl, Police Say." *Daily Press*, December 4, 1973.

"Child Safety Meeting Tonight." *Times-Union*, December 5, 1973.

"430 Call in Maenza Murder Case." *Democrat and Chronicle*, December 5, 1973.

Shore, Mike. "20 More Assigned to Slaying Probe." *Times-Union*, December 5, 1973.

"Can You Help Solve Killing?" *Times-Union*, December 6, 1973.

"Callers Keeping Two Lines Busy." *Democrat and Chronicle*, December 6, 1973.

"Open Letter to Slayer: Turn Yourself In." *Times-Union*, December 6, 1973.

Spreier, Scott. "They Want to Make Their Streets Safer." *Democrat and Chronicle*, December 6, 1973.

"160 to Discuss Children's Safety." *Times-Union*, December 6, 1973.

Goldberg, Gerald. "Police Pursue New Lead in Slaying of Girl." *Democrat and Chronicle*, December 6, 1973.

"Picture in T-U Tomorrow." *Times-Union*, December 7, 1973.

"Reward Up $800 in Slaying Case." *Democrat and Chronicle*, December 7, 1973.

"Police Post Photo to Get New Leads in Girl's Death." *Democrat and Chronicle*, December 8, 1973.

"Telephone Tips Pile Up in Slaying; Few Clues." *Times-Union*, December 10, 1973.

"Please Call, Police Urge." *Times-Union*, December 11, 1973.

"Police Working on 2 New Leads." *Times-Union*, December 11, 1973.

"Police Check New Leads in Murder." *Democrat and Chronicle*, December 11, 1973.

Marsh, Jack, and John McGinnis. "Man Quizzed, Released in Michelle Slaying." *Times-Union*, December 12, 1973.

Marsh, Jack. "Suspect, Cleared in Slaying, Spotted by Witness, Report Says." *Times-Union*, December 13, 1973.

"Suspect Quizzed in Death." *Democrat and Chronicle*, December 12, 1973.

"Police Give Suspect 'Benefit of the Doubt'." *Democrat and Chronicle*, December 13, 1973.

"Witness Line Still Receiving Calls." *Democrat and Chronicle*, December 13, 1973.

"Polygraph Test Passed by Suspect." *Daily Messenger*, December 13, 1973.

"Maenza Case Calls Wanted." *Democrat and Chronicle*, December 14, 1973.

Marsh, Jack. "Did Woman See Man at Goodman Plaza?" *Times-Union*, December 14, 1973.

Goldberg, Gerald. "3rd Maenza Witness Could Be Best Yet." *Democrat and Chronicle*, December 14, 1973.

Goldberg, Gerald. "Police Are 'Still Optimistic' They'll Solve Murder Case." *Democrat and Chronicle*, December 15, 1973.

"Still Nothing New in Slaying." *Democrat and Chronicle*, December 17, 1973.

"Slaying Leads Dwindle." *Times-Union*, December 17, 1973.

"Rape-Slayer Search Continues." *Daily Messenger*, December 18, 1973.

"Maenza Murder Case: Suspect Is Cleared." *Democrat and Chronicle*, December 22, 1973.

Buckley, Tom. "Three Rape-Murders Stir Rochester Area." *New York Times*, December 24, 1973.

"Rochester Fireman Kills Himself after He Attempted to Rape Girl." *Citizen-Advertiser*, January 2, 1974.

Goldberg, Gerald. "Police Continue Searching for Michelle's Killer." *Democrat and Chronicle*, January 12, 1974.

"Maenza Probe 'Dying.'" *Times-Union*, January 17, 1974.

Marsh, Jack. "Maenza Case: New Developments, No Breakthroughs." *Times-Union*, January 16, 1974.

Marsh, Jack. "Lombard Suggests Expanded Probe in Girls' Murders." *Times-Union*, January 18, 1974.

Shore, Mike. "Michelle's Murder Frustrates Retiring Investigator." *Times-Union*, August 1, 1974.

"Murder of Three Little Girls Confounds Rochester Police." *New York Times*, March 25, 1977.

"Another City Hunts Elusive Killers of 4." *Herald-Palladium*, March 25, 1977.

Lindsey, Robert. "Police on Coast Say They've Solved 10 of 13 'Hillside Strangler' Deaths." *New York Times*, April 24, 1979.

"Nation: Murderous Personality." *Time*, May 7, 1979.

"Wristprint May Link Him to Slayings." *Chronicle-Telegram*, August 21, 1981.

Gerew, Gary. "Bianchi Link to Slaying Here Still Hasn't Been Determined." *Democrat and Chronicle*, January 22, 1982.

"Rochester Seeks to Question Bianchi about 3 More Killings." *Daily Press*, November 12, 1983.

"Officials to Ask 'Strangler' about Local Murders." *Syracuse Herald-Journal*, November 17, 1983.

"Rochester to Question 'Hillside Strangler.'" *Syracuse Post-Standard*, November 17, 1983.

"Sheriff Suspects Slaying Linked to 'Hillside Strangler.'" *Syracuse Post-Standard*, April 27, 1984.

"Police Will Re-Examine 'Double-Initial Murders.'" *Intelligencer Record*, December 10, 1995.

Loudon, Bennett J. "'Double Initial' Deaths Retold." *Democrat and Chronicle*, May 26, 2001.

Miller, Martin. "A Dark Reflection." *Los Angeles Times*, February 27, 2002.

Connor, Tracy. "From 'Pillars' to Pervs: Net's Anonymity Cloaks Predators." *Daily News*, November 1, 2003.

"Double Initial DNA Test Clears Man." *R News*, February 21, 2007.

Bibliography

Kennedy, Helen. "DNA from Cigarette Butt May Nail '76's 'Alphabet Killer.'" *Daily News* (New York), October 4, 2007.

"Rochester Area Cops Solve Oldest Cold Case." *Democrat and Chronicle*, October 4, 2007.

"Florida Man Accused of Killing Girl in 1976." *Post-Standard*, October 4, 2007.

Craig, Gary. "'Double Initial' Murders Remain Mystery After 35 Years." *Democrat and Chronicle*, March 1, 2009.

Craig, Gary. "DNA Evidence, Tips Fuel Hunt for Killer from 1970s." *Democrat and Chronicle*, March 2, 2009.

Craig, Gary. "Serial Killer Bianchi Says He Did Not Murder 3 Girls." *Democrat and Chronicle*, March 2, 2009.

Craig, Gary. "Police Check New Leads in Old Slayings." *Democrat and Chronicle*, April 3, 2009.

Craig, Gary. "Book Aims to Stop Crimes vs. Kids." *Democrat and Chronicle*, July 10, 2009.

ONLINE SOURCES
(in order used)

"Rochester Crime Statistics and Crime Data." *Area Connect.* http://rochesterny.areaconnect.com/crime1.htm. Retrieved 12 November 2009.

"Rochester Crime Report." *Crime Statistics.* http://www.cityrating.com/citycrime.asp?city=Rochester&state=NY. Retrieved 12 November 2009.

"Rochester Population and Demographics." *Area Connect.* http://rochesterny.areaconnect.com/statistics.htm. Retrieved 12 November 2009.

"DNA Case Highlights." *New York State Division of Criminal Justice Services.* www.criminaljustice.state.ny.us/forensic/dnacasehighlights.htm. Retrieved 10 November 2009.

"DNA – Fingerprint of the 21st Century." *New York State Division of Criminal Justice Services.* www.criminaljustice.state.ny.us/forensic/index.htm. Retrieved 10 November 2009

"Accuracy of DNA 'Matches' to Definitively Identify Suspects Questioned." *Death Penalty Information Center.* http://www.deathpenaltyinfo.org/accuracy-dna-matches-definitively-identify-suspects-questioned. Retrieved 14 November 2009.

Cohen, Gail. "The History of DNA Forensics." *eHow.* www.ehow.com/about_5124338_history-dna-forensics.html. Retrieved 23 October 2009.

"History of Forensics." *History of Forensics.* http://historyofforensics.com/. Retrieved 23 October 2009.

"Results for Serial Killers from the 60s and 70s." *Fun Trivia.* www.funtrivia.com/submitquiz.cfm?quiz=178362.

"History for Rochester, NY, Friday, November 16, 1971." *Weather Underground.*
www.wunderground.com/history/airport/KROC/1971/11/16/DailyHistory.html. Retrieved 15 October 2009.

"History for Rochester, NY, Sunday, November 18, 1971." *Weather Underground.*
www.wunderground.com/history/airport/KROC/1973/11/16/DailyHistory.html. Retrieved 15 October 2009.

"Woman Raped in Washington Park, 100s Watched No One Helped." *Digg.* http://digg.com/people/Woman_Raped_in_Washington_Park_100s_Watched_No_One_Helped. Retrieved 17 June 2009.

Craig, Gary, and Max Schulte. "Double Initial Murders" interactive special report. *Democrat and Chronicle.* http://www.democratandchronicle.com/apps/pbcs.dll/section?Category=SPECIALS84. Retrieved 15 June 2009.

Bibliography

"Pedophiles and Their Characteristics." *Child Safe Tips.* http://child safetips.abouttips.com/pedophiles-and-their-characteristics .php. Retrieved 11 September 2009.

Hall, Ryan C. W., and Richard C. W. Hall. "A Profile of Pedophilia: Definition, Characteristics of Offenders, Recidivism, Treatment Outcomes, and Forensic Issues." *Mayo Clinic Proceedings.* www.mayoclinicproceedings.com/content/82/4/457.full. Retrieved 14 November 2009.

"Ramsey discussion 2." *Webb Sleuths.* www.webbsleuths.org/ cgi-bin/dcforum/dcboard.cgi. Retrieved 6 November 2009.

Radel, F. Robert II. "Profiles of Sexual Predators and Reducing the Risk of Sexual Misconduct at Your Church, School or Other Youth Organization." www.butlerpappas.com/showarticle .aspx?Show=1416. Retrieved 6 November 2009.

"History for Rochester, NY, Monday, April 2, 1973." *Weather Underground.* www.wunderground.com/history/airport/KROC/1973/ 4/2/DailyHistory.html. Retrieved 15 October 2009.

"History for Rochester, NY, Monday, April 3, 1973." *Weather Underground.* www.wunderground.com/history/airport/KROC/1973/ 4/3/DailyHistory.html. Retrieved 15 October 2009.

"70s Fads." *Super 70s.* http://super70s.com/Community/forums/ 1189/ShowForum.aspx. Retrieved 15 October 2009.

"PolandBorderSurnames-Obituaries-L Archives." *Roots Web.* http://listsearches.rootsweb.com/th/read/PolandBorder Surnames-OBITUARIES/2003-06/... Retrieved 19 October 2009.

"1973 Potpourri." *1970s Flashback.* www.1970sflashback.com/ 1973/Potpourri.asp. Retrieved 15 October 2009.

"History for Rochester, NY, Monday, November 26, 1973." *Weather Underground.* www.wunderground.com/history/airport/ KROC/1973/11/26/DailyHistory.html. Retrieved 15 October 2009.

"History for Rochester, NY, Wednesday, November 28, 1973." *Weather Underground.* www.wunderground.com/history/airport/KROC/1973/11/28/DailyHistory.html. Retrieved 15 October 2009.

"Registered Sex Offenders by County as of November 9, 2009." *New York State Division of Criminal Justice Services.* www.criminal justice.state.ny.us/nsor/stat_by_county.htm. Retrieved 10 November 2009.

"Frequently Asked Questions." *New York State Division of Criminal Justice Services.* www.criminaljustice.state.ny.us/nsor/faq.htm. Retrieved 10 November 2009.

"Generalized Characteristics of Serial Murderers." *Criminal Profiling Research.* www.criminalprofiling.ch/character.html. Retrieved 6 November 2009.

Brown, Pat. "Serial Killer Myths Exposed." *Tru TV.* www.truetv.com/library/crime/criminal_mind/profiling/s_k_myths/4.html. Retrieved 6 November 2009.

Winerman, Lea. "Criminal Profiling: The Reality Behind the Myth." *APA Online.* www.apa.org/monitor/julaug04/criminal.html. Retrieved 23 October 2009.

Kyle. "Angelo Buono – Kenneth Bianchi." *Buono/Bianchi.* http://library.thinkquest.org/04oct/00803/BuonoBianchi.htm. Retrieved 15 June 2009.

Trekmate. "Hillside Serial Murderers." *Trek Serial Killers.* http://trekmateserialkillers.blogspot.com/2007/09/hillside-serial-murderers.html. Retrieved 12 June 2009.

Hooper, Riley. "Killers Close to Home." *The Occidental Weekly.* http://media.www.oxyweekly.com/media/storage/paper1200/news/2008/03/21/Features/Killers.Close.To.Home-3277826.shtml. Retrieved 4 November 2009.

Snyder, Steven. "The Alphabet Killer." *Metromix Rochester.* http://rochester.metromix.com/events/article/the-alphabet-killer/749678/content. Retrieved 5 November 2009.

"Statistics." *Diocese of Rochester.* http://www.catholic-hierarchy.org/diocese/droch.html. Retrieved 5 November 2009.

"People Living in Poverty." *Act Rochester.* www.actrochester.org/Indicator/Default.aspx?id=7&indicator=60. Retrieved 4 November 2009.

"Rochester City, New York." *U.S. Census Bureau American FactFinder.* http://factfinder.census.gov/servlet/ACSSAFFFacts?_event=Search&geo_id=&_geoContext=&_street=&_county=rochester&_cityTown=rochester&_state=04000US36&_zip=&_lang=en&_sse=on&pctxt=fph&pgsl=010. Retrieved 26 October 2009.

"IQ Tests Can Be Wrong: The Story of Gregory Ochoa." *Audioblox.* http://iq-test.learninginfo.org/iq06.htm. Retrieved 4 November 2009.

"Missing Person: Sharon Shechter." *Monroe County Sheriff's Office Crime Stoppers.* www.monroecountysheriff.info/crimestop/unsolved.html. Retrieved 16 June 2009.

Denise. "Re: Missing Woman: Sandra Sollie – NY – 5/23/94." *Project Jason.* www.projectjason.org/forums/index.php?topic=479.0;topicseen. Retrieved 16 June 2009.

"Mary Ann Wesolowski." *MPCCN.* www.angelfire.com/mi3/mpccn/wesolowski.html. Retrieved 26 October 2009

"Case File 1UFNY." *The Doe Network.* www.doenetwork.org/cases/1ufny.html. Retrieved 26 October 2009.

"Investigative Programs Critical Incident Response Group." *Federal Bureau of Investigation.* www.fbi.gov/hq/isd/cirg/ncavc.htm#vicap. Retrieved 26 October 2009.

"The Connecticut Cases." *Official Cold Case Investigations.* http://officialcoldcaseinvestigations.com/showthread.php?t=1538. Retrieved 26 October 2009.

"Lisa Joy White." *Web Sleuths*. www.websleuths.com/forums/
archive/index.php/t-31454.html. Retrieved 26 October 2009.

"Lisa Joy White." *I Care Missing Persons Cold Cases*. http://icare
missingpersonscoldcases.yuku.com/topic/404. Retrieved 26
October 2009.

Gado, Mark. "Robert Garrow." *truTV*. www.trutv.com/library/
crime/serial_killers/predators/robert_garrow/2.html. Retrieved
9 November 2009.

cHodge. "Re: Any Info on Janice Pocket Case from the 1970's." *Cold
Case Files Discussions*. http://boards.aetv.com/topic/Do-You
-Have/Any-Info-On/100003422. Retrieved 26 October 2009.

"What is the AMBER Alert System?" *NYS AMBER*. http://amber
.ny.gov/. Retrieved 10 November 2009.

"Operation SAFE CHILD." *New York State Division of Criminal
Justice*. www.criminaljustice.state.ny.us/pio/safechild.htm.
Retrieved 10 November 2009.

"Missing Kids." *National Center for Missing & Exploited Children*.
www.missingkids.com. Retrieved 9 November 2009.

About the Author

Cheri Farnsworth, under the name Cheri Revai, is the author of *The Big Book of New York Ghost Stories* and four other titles in Stackpole's Haunted Series: *Haunted Massachusetts, Haunted Connecticut, Haunted New York*, and *Haunted New York City*. She is also the author of the true crime titles *Adirondack Enigma* and *Murder and Mayhem in St. Lawrence County*.

Farnsworth lives in upstate New York with her husband, daughters, and a houseful of pets. She enjoys researching regional history, true crime, and the paranormal. Her Web site at www.cherifarnsworth.com provides more information on her books and upcoming projects.